Ancient Astrology

The Ultimate Guide to Babylonian, Egyptian, and Hellenistic Astrology and the Zodiac Signs

© Copyright 2023 - All rights reserved.

The content contained within this book may not be reproduced, duplicated, or transmitted without direct written permission from the author or the publisher.

Under no circumstances will any blame or legal responsibility be held against the publisher, or author, for any damages, reparation, or monetary loss due to the information contained within this book, either directly or indirectly.

Legal Notice:

This book is copyright protected. It is only for personal use. You cannot amend, distribute, sell, use, quote, or paraphrase any part, or the content within this book, without the consent of the author or publisher.

Disclaimer Notice:

Please note the information contained within this document is for educational and entertainment purposes only. All effort has been executed to present accurate, up-to-date, reliable, and complete information. No warranties of any kind are declared or implied. Readers acknowledge that the author is not engaging in the rendering of legal, financial, medical, or professional advice. The content within this book has been derived from various sources. Please consult a licensed professional before attempting any techniques outlined in this book.

By reading this document, the reader agrees that under no circumstances is the author responsible for any losses, direct or indirect, that are incurred as a result of the use of the information contained within this document, including, but not limited to, errors, omissions, or inaccuracies.

Your Free Gift
(Only available for a limited time)

Thanks for getting this book! If you want to learn more about various spirituality topics, then join Mari Silva's community and get a free guided meditation MP3 for awakening your third eye. This guided meditation mp3 is designed to open and strengthen ones third eye so you can experience a higher state of consciousness. Simply visit the link below the image to get started.

https://spiritualityspot.com/meditation

Table of Contents

INTRODUCTION 1
CHAPTER 1: INTRODUCTION TO ANCIENT ASTROLOGY 3
CHAPTER 2: THE FIVE WANDERING STARS AND THE TWO LIGHTS 12
CHAPTER 3: BABYLON: WHERE ASTROLOGY WAS BORN 22
CHAPTER 4: EGYPTIAN ASTROLOGY AND THE DECANS 31
CHAPTER 5: THE EGYPTIAN ZODIAC SIGNS 42
CHAPTER 6: HELLENISTIC ASTROLOGY I. THE TOPOI 59
CHAPTER 7: HELLENISTIC ASTROLOGY II. THE ZOIDIA 67
CHAPTER 8: THE THEMA MUNDI AND HELLENISTIC CHARTS 75
CHAPTER 9: THE HERMETIC LOTS 82
CHAPTER 10: ANCIENT HELLENISTIC TECHNIQUES 90
CHAPTER 11: MAKE YOUR OWN ASTROLABE 96
CONCLUSION 100
BONUS: GLOSSARY OF ASTROLOGICAL TERMS 102
HERE'S ANOTHER BOOK BY MARI SILVA THAT YOU MIGHT LIKE 108
YOUR FREE GIFT (ONLY AVAILABLE FOR A LIMITED TIME) 109
REFERENCES 110

Introduction

Astrology is an ancient field of study that holds great significance in almost every civilization known to man. Whether we realize it or not, it plays a major role in our life, affecting and even explaining our past, present, and future. Astrology gives us a better understanding of who we are and how people see us. It can help us understand our dreams, aspirations, behaviors, needs, and emotions. Reading into astrology can help us elevate numerous aspects of life. It gives us insight into the type of career we should pursue based on how we approach professional relationships, our level of financial security, our natural talents, etc. Astrology can also help us cultivate healthier and stronger relationships because it grants us a deeper understanding of what we expect to receive from others. Not to mention that it helps us understand the personalities and behaviors of those around us.

Astrology is also widely used as a form of divination. Many rely on planetary movements and placements to predict the future and avoid any potential mishaps. It's not much of a surprise that so many people are fascinated by the movement of celestial bodies, whether they read the daily horoscope section in their favorite magazine for fun or turn to astrology for guidance regarding the numerous aspects of their lives, including financial, career-related, wellness, or relationships.

Centuries ago, the sciences of astronomy and astrology went hand-in-hand, further denoting just how important this method of divination was. The study of astrology was first developed in Mesopotamia, where it eventually made its way into India and then Greece during the Hellenistic period. Islamic regions adopted this study as a Greek tradition, where it was learned in Arabic before being passed on to Europe once more. The Chinese also held astrology in the highest regard, where each newborn child was given a horoscope. Horoscopes were also part of the standard procedure when a person had an important decision to make in life. Many people today still believe that astrology significantly influences our personalities.

By reading this book, you'll learn all about astrology's origins and how numerous ancient cultures and their understanding of the study influenced the astrological system we know today. In the final chapter, you'll find step-by-step instructions on how you can make your own Astrolabe. This book is not only interesting, but it also includes an abundance of indispensable information. It is perfect for beginners and experts alike.

Chapter 1: Introduction to Ancient Astrology

Over the last 200 years, astrology has gained a renewed popularity in the West. While many parts of the world have continued to place great importance on astrology over the centuries, its popularity has diminished since the Enlightenment. However, a combination of interest in spiritualism and New Age philosophy in the 19th century led to astrology's development and evolution to what we know today.

However, there's much more to astrology than simply the modern version we know today - there are also several ancient versions still in practice, and these have their own benefits. Suppose you've ever found yourself curious about ancient astrology. In that case, you're in the right place - this book is the perfect way to learn more about Babylonian, Hellenistic, and Egyptian astrology.

Understanding Modern Astrology

Before exploring ancient astrology, it's important to understand modern astrology in further detail.

When we say "modern astrology," we generally mean modern Western astrology. Chinese, East Asian, and Hindu astrological traditions are significantly different and are often unrecognizable to even the most ardent disciples of modern Western astrology.

This form of astrology is generally considered a form of divination and is most commonly based on a person's natal chart. The natal chart is created based on the exact time of a person's birth and consists of a chart of the sky as it appeared at that exact moment.

In modern Western astrology, the distance between the Sun and the Earth is one of the most important astrological calculations. Modern astrology also emphasizes which of the 12 signs a person is born under. This is determined based on a person's date of birth, and the 12 signs are:

- The Ram (Aries)
- The Bull (Taurus)
- The Twins (Gemini)
- The Crab (Cancer)
- The Lion (Leo)
- The Virgin (Virgo)
- The Scales (Libra)
- The Scorpion (Scorpio)
- The Centaur (Sagittarius)
- The Sea-Goat (Capricorn)
- The Water-Bearer (Aquarius)
- The Fish (Pisces)

Zodiac signs also determine the 12 spatial divisions of a person's natal chart. When analyzed, the movements and positions of the Sun, Moon, and other planetary bodies help astrologers make predictions.

However, it should be noted that the most common form of modern Western astrology is a simpler version of natal chart readings. These take the form of horoscopes, which are concerned only about the zodiac sign under which a person is born. This determination only makes up about 1/12th of a traditional natal chart, which is a significantly more detailed and in-depth analysis of the life and future of a person.

Astrology's popularity among esotericists is this high because it not only influenced them, but also practitioners of Wicca, Hermeticism, and other similar belief systems. Some scholars went as far as to claim that all magicians have at least a rudimentary familiarity with astrology. The practice is as important as tarot divination regarding public perception of Western magical systems.

One of the most important elements of modern astronomy is its ability to change and evolve with new discoveries. As you'll discover in this book, several planets were unknown during the period of the ancient astrologists, and thus these traditions do not use these planetary bodies in the astrological readings. At the same time, it's also essential to remember that this does not mean that further understanding of ancient astrology is not worth it.

The Reasons behind Modern Astrology's Popularity

Understanding the popularity of modern astrology can be challenging, especially for people who do not believe in it. However, there are several reasons behind this phenomenon.

The simplest answer to this question is that astrology promises answers to your questions. By reading your natal chart, you can find a resolution to long-seated questions that may have been hampering your ability to live a happy and fulfilling life.

Additionally, the advent of the internet means that astrology is more accessible than ever. In the past, creating a birth chart for a client (or yourself) would require familiarity with various other subjects, including astronomy and geometry. It is simple to create your own birth chart with many online tools at your disposal so long as you have the time, location, and date of the birth. Thus, if you're interested in working as an astrologist, you only need to know how to analyze a person's natal chart, not how to build it.

Furthermore, astrology services are easy to access. Some apps offer quick, short readings, and you can also find astrologers willing to perform personalized readings easily online. Suppose you cannot find someone who lives near you and can perform an in-person reading. In that case, you can just as easily find a qualified astrologer who operates over Zoom.

One theory holds that another major reason for the resurgence in popularity of astrology and other similar mystical practices is that people feel like they no longer have control over their own lives. People no longer feel more conscious than ever of how circumstances outside their control affect how their life unfolds. Astrology returns some sense of control to people, as they can look at their fate and act accordingly to ensure they either avoid or meet with it.

Astrology essentially offers the possibility for self-determination and self-interpretation, which is also part of the reason it is so popular among marginalized communities. For example, it has found a home among the LGBTQ community, millennials who fear what the future holds for their generation, and those affected by major events such as the COVID-19 pandemic and the Black Lives Matter movement. These events can leave many people feeling out of sorts and questioning their place in a changing world, and astrology answers those questions.

Benefits of Astrology

If you're only dipping your feet into the vast pond that is astrology, you may find yourself wondering what the benefits of this practice are. This is especially true when you're looking at a particular form of astrology like modern astrology. You may even wonder why you should learn about modern astrology before moving on to ancient astrological traditions. Some benefits include:

- A detailed natal chart can provide you with a psychological road map and a compass for the rest of your life, offering you a sense of direction and purpose, especially if you feel lost.
- You are offered a new worldview, allowing you to see the world around you from a new angle. This can help you move past negative emotions, such as pain, fear, and trauma, and move forward on your journey through life.
- A natal chart reading can help you better understand yourself. It helps you think back on the circumstances of your life and understand whether there are actions you should be taking and opportunities you have been avoiding

that you should be meeting.

- Astrology can help you understand specific facets of your overall existence. Aside from general natal chart readings, several branches of modern astrology exist. These give you a better understanding of various facets of your life, including how to interact with financial markets, the effects of astrology on medical issues, how to use it to understand your romantic and platonic relationships better, and more.
- Learning how to perform astrological readings will also help you better understand people with different personality types. This will enable you to work more effectively with the people around you and help you adapt to their strengths and weaknesses. It will make you a better friend, partner, listener, and confidant.

Understanding Ancient Astrology

So far, we've covered modern astrology in great detail. However, there's far more to the history of astrology than simply the version we know today.

Astrology was practiced extensively across a range of ancient civilizations. The type of astrology they practiced often differed from place to place, which is why Chinese astrology is markedly different from Indian astrology, which is, in turn, very different from Western astrology.

However, some astrological traditions were connected - specifically, Babylonian, Egyptian, and Hellenistic astrology. Due to this connective thread, these three types of astrology are collectively known as ancient astrology.

Babylonian Astrology

Babylonian astrology is the oldest known form of organized astrology and dates back to at least the second millennium BC. The oldest detailed texts on Babylonian astrology are a set of 32 tablets that date back to approximately 1875 BC.

The Babylonians used horoscopic astrology, and these horoscopes were created based on observing the seasonal movements of the fixed stars and the known planets (there were five known planets - Jupiter, Venus, Saturn, Mercury, and Mars), the

Sun, and the Moon. They believed that the actions of the gods influenced human lives, which took the form of the movement of celestial objects.

Aside from using astrology as a form of future divination, it was also an important part of the practice of astral medicine. This practice involved the creation of different remedies for different days and dates.

Astrology also helped influence the calendar creation for the following year, including when festivals and important religious activities were scheduled.

Egyptian Astrology

Egyptian astrology shares some similarities with Babylonian astrology. In 525 BC, the Persians conquered Egypt. During the 1st century BC, the Dendera zodiac was inscribed as a base relief on a ceiling in the Hathor temple at Dendera. It is one of the best-preserved ancient depictions of the stars and celestial objects visible to the people at the time. Two signs of this zodiac – the Balance and the Scorpion – are the same as in Babylonian and Mesopotamian astrology.

However, the more prominent form of Egyptian astrology was Decanic astrology. This form of astrology uses 36 groups of stars and constellations to divide the 360-degree eclipse into 36 equal parts. This gave way to a split of the day into two 12-hour halves. This would change over the seasons, with night and day becoming longer and shorter in relation to each other. The Egyptians also used it to mark the divisions of their solar calendars.

Following the conquest of Egypt by Alexander the Great in 332 BC, Babylonian astrology was combined with this earlier form of Decanic astrology to form the first type of horoscopic astrology. This form of astrology likely led to the creation of the Dendera zodiac.

The Egyptian zodiac featured 12 zodiac signs, each based on a particular god or goddess.

Hellenistic Astrology

Hellenistic astrology is a form of astrology that was first developed during the late 2nd century or early 1st century BC. The texts on this were written mainly in Greek or Latin, and it was practiced in and around the Mediterranean Basin, especially in Egypt, Greece, and Rome.

This type of astrology is a tradition of horoscopic astrology that combined the Babylonian zodiac with the Egyptian tradition of Decanic astrology and the Greek system of planetary gods, the four elements (earth, air, water, and fire), and the rule of the zodiac signs over certain parts of a horoscope. The originator of this form of astronomy is unknown, but some sources name him the legendary sage Hermes Trismegistus.

This type of astrology was the first of the major Western astrology traditions to focus on an individual's natal chart. It used the ascendent signs and 12 celestial houses that are still in use today. Indeed, Hellenistic astrology remains remarkably similar to modern astrology, despite the many changes and evolutions the latter has undergone.

Ancient Astrology vs. Modern Astrology

Given that, as mentioned above, Hellenistic astrology is remarkably similar to modern astrology, you may wonder if there are truly any differences between the two.

The simple answer is yes, there are.

Perhaps the most prominent difference is the fact that ancient astrologers only made use of five planets (Jupiter, Venus, Saturn, Mercury, and Mars), the Sun, and the Moon in their predictions. These were occasionally also known as the seven planets. Uranus, Neptune, and Pluto, which the naked eye cannot see, had not yet been discovered and would not be for over 1000 years (Uranus was discovered in 1781, Neptune in 1846, and Pluto in 1930). These three planets are used in modern astrology despite being understandably nonexistent in ancient traditions.

Additionally, ancient astrology features several theoretical models, making it more challenging for people to learn. Modern astrology is comparatively easier to learn, especially the basics.

Furthermore, modern astrology is far more focused on the psychology of the individual who is being given a reading. While ancient astrology also featured natal chart readings, these were more aimed at exploring how society saw you, your place in society, and what you could do to change that place if you desired.

Modern astrology subscribes to free will, and you can transcend the tendencies seen in your natal chart through hard work. Ancient astrology, however, has a much more essentialist view of the individual and the world, and readings focus more on helping you understand your place in the world than on helping you transcend the will of fate.

The easiest way to think of this difference between modern and ancient astrology is that, while modern astrology focuses on a person's inner world, ancient astrology places far more importance on the outside world. This is best seen in Babylonian astrology. This form of ancient astrology focused primarily on determining events that were of public importance and affected the general welfare of the population of the state at large. An individual's interests were generally unimportant when making astrological predictions. It would take several centuries and the development of Hellenistic astrology until the individual horoscope truly became popular.

Why You Should Study Ancient Astrology

Given the differences between ancient and modern astrology, you may wonder whether it's worth studying the former. After all, modern astrology offers numerous effective insights into a person's natal chart, and ancient astrology can often seem far more challenging and time-consuming to learn.

However, there are benefits to gaining a better understanding of ancient astrology. For one, ancient astrology is essentially the history of modern astrology, and understanding the evolution from one to the other will give you a better insight into modern astrology.

At the same time, there are changes from ancient to modern astrology that many people feel negatively affect how horoscopes are analyzed. Often, important analytical elements were lost due to politics. For example, some key features of Hellenistic astrology fell out of use not because they were ineffective but because of suspicions that Arabs invented these.

Additionally, ancient astrology is focused on a far more realistic interpretation of an individual's chart. Modern astrology tends to view all charts as equally lucky and believes that everyone has an equal chance of being successful in life. Ancient astrology is more realistic in that it acknowledges that some charts are luckier than others, allowing the astrologer to interpret the chart in question in a way that isn't setting up the client for disappointment.

Modern astrology focuses on the internal self, which means that it can often fall behind when exploring your chart's impact on your material life. However, ancient astrology is cognizant that your material life is important and does not shy away from exploring both the positives and negatives of your natal chart, ensuring you are properly prepared for the journey ahead.

If you're hoping to learn more about ancient astrology, you're in the right place. All you need to do is keep reading. This book will cover all three types of ancient astrology (Babylonian, Egyptian, and Hellenistic) in further detail and give you a better understanding of their similarities and differences compared to modern astrology.

You'll also learn to make your own astrolabe, which you can then use when performing astrological readings. Astrolabes were an essential tool for Hellenistic astrologers, and having one with you when you conduct your readings will help you take your practice to the next level. Finally, there will be a bonus glossary of astrological terms, which will serve as an easy reference you can return to at any time during your journey.

Chapter 2: The Five Wandering Stars and the Two Lights

The ancient Greeks were one of the very few cultures that played a huge role in shaping ancient astrology that paved the road to the modern astrology we know today. In fact, many of the terms used in astrology have Greek origins. For instance, the words "planet" and "star" are always front and center when discussing zodiac signs or anything related to the topic. "Planet" is derived from the ancient Greek word planētēs which means "wanderers," while "star" is derived from the Greek word astēr.

The planet symbols.
Macalves, CC BY-SA 3.0 <https://creativecommons.org/licenses/by-sa/3.0>, via Wikimedia Commons https://commons.wikimedia.org/wiki/File:Planets_symbols.png

By observing the night sky, the ancient Greeks discovered five planets out of the eight ones in the solar system since they were bright and close enough to be seen with the naked eye. This includes Venus, Mercury, Jupiter, Mars, and Saturn—also known as the "wandering stars," or *astēr planētēs*. The ancient Greeks chose the name "wandering stars" because these planets wandered from their path, unlike the "fixed stars" that appear in the same arrangement in the sky every night. The rest of the planets were discovered centuries later after the invention of the telescope.

It wasn't just the ancient Greeks who were fascinated with the "wandering stars." The ancient Babylonians were also known to record the cycles of these five planets because they were curious about their positions in the sky, even assigning meanings to these positions. The people of ancient times did more than just study these heavenly bodies—the moon and the sun were tracked too, and their movements were observed. They were referred to as the two lights or the luminaries, derived from the Late Latin word luminarium, which means light.

The ancient Greeks, Babylonians, Egyptians, Sumerians, Indians, Chinese, and other ancient cultures associated the planets with some of their gods and goddesses. Each of the five wandering stars was named thousands of years ago after either an ancient goddess or god, with each name having a specific meaning and relating to the type of energy each planet gives.

Planets are divided into two categories in astrology: benefic and malefic. Benefic planets usually have a more positive influence on the horoscope and birth chart than malefic planets, which usually have a negative or bad influence. Benefic planets mean pleasant surprises are coming your way, while malefic planets indicate challenging times. That said, the terms malefic and benefic don't have a huge influence in Western astrology as they do in ancient Greek and Vedic astrology. However, familiarizing yourself with the concept will help you better understand astrological transits and your birth chart.

So which planets are benefic? Which planets are malefic? What is the secret behind each planet's name? You'll find the answers to these questions and more in this chapter.

Mercury

Mercury is the first planet in the solar system and the closest one to the Sun. It is a small planet. You may have heard the term "Mercury retrograde" before. That is a phenomenon that occurs when planets spin backward around the Sun. You are probably thinking, can planets orbit in reverse? Well, not exactly. The planets don't move in reverse per se; it is more of an optical illusion that makes them seem like they do. In reality, the Earth is spinning faster as it finishes its orbit around the Sun. Since we are the ones moving faster, it seems that the planets are moving backward when observed from the Earth.

Although all planets retrograde, Mercury's retrograde is the most common and discussed one. This is because the planet retrogrades about three or four times each year, which can negatively affect our lives. Astrologers believe that when planets retrograde, we can feel its impact on ourselves and every aspect of our lives. Since Mercury rules our communication skills, so you may struggle to find the right words for days or weeks. You may even experience arguments and misunderstandings more often during it.

What Deities Are Associated with Mercury?

Mercury was named after the Roman messenger of the gods with the same name, who was also the god of merchants and travelers. Unlike Earth, it only takes Mercury 88 days to rotate around the Sun, making it the fastest solar planet. This makes the name Mercury perfect for this planet since the Roman God Mercury has wings which make him very fast.

The planet is associated with Mercury's counterpart in Greek mythology, Hermes, who was also the messenger of the gods. Mercury is also associated with the ancient Egyptian god Djehuty (or Thoth as referred to by the Greeks), who was also the messenger of the gods and invented writing and languages. The association with the god Djehuty is befitting since Mercury rules over our communication skills and thought processes. The planet is also associated with the Babylonian messenger of the gods Nabu, the god of literature, scribe, and wisdom.

Is Mercury Benefic or Malefic?
Mercury is considered a benefic planet.

What Is Mercury Known As?
Mercury is known as the glistening one because it is one of the brightest objects in the sky.

What Does Mercury Do?
Mercury rules over communication skills, intellect, and memory. It is the lens you see the world through. It serves as a messenger, just like the gods it is associated with and helps you deliver your words and thoughts to others. You can learn a lot about a person by talking and communicating, so Mercury can help a person make a strong first impression. It is through this planet that we establish connections with other people.

What Is the Energy of Mercury Known For?
Mercury represents mental energy and intelligence. It also helps us make declarations and say what is on our minds. Simply put, Mercury's energy helps us communicate our thoughts and feelings.

In Which Sign Is Mercury Exalted?
Virgo.

In Which Sign Is Mercury Depressed?
Pisces.

N.B. *To better understand what it means for a planet to be exalted or depressed, look at the glossary at the end of the book.*

Venus

Venus is two places from the sun. It is one of the brightest heavenly bodies in the night sky. The planet can be seen with the naked eye right before dawn and just before sunset. For this reason, the ancient Egyptians and Greeks mistook Venus for two planets. They referred to one as the morning star and the other as the evening star. It wasn't until the Hellenistic period discovered that it was actually one planet.

What Deities Are Associated with Venus?
Venus was the Roman goddess of beauty and romance or love. Unlike all the other planets named after male deities, Venus is the

only planet named after a goddess. In Greek mythology, Venus is associated with Aphrodite, the goddess of love and beauty. Its Egyptian counterpart Isis is the goddess of love, magic, motherhood, and fertility. In Babylonian mythology, the planet is associated with the goddess of sexual love and war, Ishtar.

As one of the brightest and most beautiful planets, it is no wonder it was named after goddesses associated with love and beauty. Venus also has a feminine mystique and features.

Is Venus Benefic or Malefic?

Venus is considered a benefic planet as it positively impacts your interpersonal relationships and supports your interactions with the people in your life.

What Is Venus Known As?

Venus is known as the "morning star" or "evening star," as mentioned above. As the shiniest planet in the sky, Venus is known for its exceptional brightness because the planet's surface reflects most of its sunlight into space. It is also one of the closest planets to Earth, making it easy to see it shining in the sky. Venus is also referred to as Earth's twin since they resemble one another in density and size.

What Does Venus Do?

Venus rules over love, beauty, adoration, pleasure, and luxury. The planet also guides us in approaching love, romance, affection, relationships, and sensual pleasures. Venus is associated with charm, grace, and our love for art. Simply put, whatever makes us happy, is associated with this planet. It is through Venus that you feel attracted to other people and things like a job or a car. Venus also brings harmony and peace to your life.

What Is the Energy of Venus Known For?

Venus's energy impacts aesthetics, creativity, fashion, knowledge, wisdom, and feminine energy.

In Which Sign Is Venus Exalted?

Pisces.

In Which Sign Is Venus Depressed?

Virgo.

Mars

Mars is the fourth planet from the Sun and is considered very close to Earth. Unlike the feminine planet Venus, Mars is associated with masculinity which is where the title of the popular book "Men are from Mars, Women are from Venus" came from.

What Deities Are Associated with Mars?

Mars is named after the Roman god of war, Mars. In Greek mythology, the planet is named after the Greek god of war, Ares, who was Aphrodite's husband. Two moons circle Mars—Deimos, meaning 'dread,' and Phobos, meaning 'fear,' both of whom are sons of Ares, the Roman god. Ares had a chariot called "the chariot of terror" that he often rode with his sons Deimos and Phobos. In ancient Egypt, Mars was called Har Decher, the red one, while the Babylonians called it Nergal, meaning the god of war, death, fire, and destruction.

Ancient cultures associated Mars with war, destruction, and bloodshed due to the planet's red color, which is the same color as blood.

Is Mars Benefic or Malefic?

Mars is a malefic planet. There is no surprise here for a planet associated with war, blood, and death. Mars can interfere with the good things in your life by adding tension and negativity.

What Is Mars Known As?

Mars is known as the red planet. The reason behind the planet's red color is that it contains a lot of rocks that are full of iron. When the rocks and the planet's surface area are exposed to various weather factors, they oxidize and turn into a sort of red color.

What Does Mars Do?

Mars rules over our survival instinct, anger, and aggression. This planet is what drives you into action and adventure and pushes you to get out of bed every morning. Mars is also associated with attraction, but it differs from its more romantic counterpart, Venus. While Venus focuses on establishing deeper and romantic connections, Mars focuses on physical attraction.

What Is the Energy of Mars Known For?
Mars's energy is masculinity and fulfilling sexual desire.

In Which Sign Is Mars Exalted?
Capricorn.

In Which Sign Is Mars Depressed?
Cancer.

Jupiter

Jupiter is the fifth planet from the Sun and the largest planet in the solar system.

What Deities Associated with Jupiter?

Jupiter was named after the Roman king of gods Jupiter, a name that fits the largest planet in the solar system. The Greeks named Jupiter Zeus, their king of gods and god of the sky, and he is also one of the most popular gods in modern times. In ancient Egypt, Jupiter was associated with the god of the air Amun, one of the most powerful and primordial Egyptian gods. The Babylonians called Jupiter after their chief god Marduk. As the largest planet in the solar system, Jupiter is associated with the most powerful deities in each culture.

Is Jupiter Benefic or Malefic?

Jupiter is a benefic planet as it brings good fortune and supports all the positive steps you take in your life.

What Is Jupiter Known As?

Jupiter is known as the largest planet in the solar system. It is also known for its stripes and its Giant Red Spot. The planet is covered with thick clouds of different colors, which often resemble stripes, while its Giant Red Spot results from a giant spinning storm.

What Does Jupiter Do?

Jupiter has a powerful impact on zodiac signs due to its massive size. For starters, it helps you better understand yourself and your personality. It is believed Jupiter's impact can affect your financial life and can even make people rich. The planet rules over wisdom, knowledge, and dedication and helps you connect with your spiritual side. Jupiter is the planet of luck and can bring good fortune and prosperity into someone's life. It is also associated with various positive qualities like hope, honor, gratitude, new possibilities, growth, goodwill, mercy, generosity, tolerance, and a sense of humor.

What Is the Energy of Jupiter Known For?

Jupiter's energy is about compassion, optimism, generosity, and hope. This planet can be compared to a guardian angel that guides you using its energy to lead a happier and more fulfilling life.

In Which Sign Is Jupiter Exalted?

Cancer.

In Which Sign Is Jupiter Depressed?

Capricorn.

Saturn

Saturn is second in size to Jupiter and is the sixth planet from the Sun.

What Deities Are Associated with Saturn?

Saturn was named after the Roman god of wealth, agriculture, and time Saturnus who is also the father of Jupiter. The Greeks named this planet after Cronus, who was the youngest of the six Titans, the god of time, and the father of Zeus. The ancient Egyptians called Saturn Geb - the god of the earth - while the Babylonians called Ninurta the god of farming and healing. Saturn is the slowest planet of all the wandering stars; it takes 29 years to orbit the Sun. For this reason, it is believed it was called Saturn and Cronus after the gods of time in both Roman and Greek cultures.

Is Saturn Benefic or Malefic?

Saturn is a malefic planet. Many people are haunted by their past. It can be baggage they must constantly carry to be reminded of how heavy their burden is; this baggage is Saturn's presence in your birth chart.

What Is Saturn Known As?

Saturn is the second-largest planet in the solar system after Jupiter. It is also a unique planet due to the beautiful rings surrounding it. Although other planets have rings like Jupiter, none of them can be compared to Saturn's. Saturn has seven rings made of rocks and ice, and each ring orbits the planet independently.

It is believed that Saturn didn't always have its rings, but millions of years ago, it had a large moon orbiting it. The faster this moon moved, the faster it got close to the planet until it was pulled in two different directions simultaneously. This resulted in a huge explosion, and the remains formed what we know now as the Saturn rings. The remains are still falling on the planet into space to this day. It is believed that they will keep falling until the rings completely disappear.

What Does Saturn Do?

You can think of Saturn as a strict parent that brings discipline, structure, rules, and obligation into your life. It also constantly reminds us of our commitments and responsibilities and how we should set healthy boundaries. It rules over wisdom, expertise, and time. The planet is also associated with karma and wisdom. We can all benefit from learning lessons in life that can help us grow. Saturn helps open your eyes to the areas in your life that need working on so you can finally grow. This planet is all about taking small steps, patience, and persistence due to being one of the slowest planets.

Like a strict parent, Saturn will provide tough love to help you mature and grow into the person you are supposed to be. It can also be a force behind you to help you face your fears. Simply put, Saturn will push you out of your comfort zone so you can change, grow, and become the best version of yourself.

What Is the Energy of Saturn Known For?

Saturn's energy is related to limitations and restrictions. However, you shouldn't see this energy in a negative light. It is meant to help you grow and become wiser and more **experienced.**

In Which Sign Is Saturn Exalted?

Libra.

In Which Sign Is Saturn Depressed?

Aries.

The wandering stars have been a fascinating topic since ancient times and up till this day. We can learn so much about our personality by following these stars and understanding their positions and movements. The ancient Greeks, Egyptians, and Babylonians contributed a lot to astrology by observing the night skies. Observing the stars and their impact on your life can help you learn more about what each planet offers to your sign and how they can impact various areas in your life.

Chapter 3: Babylon: Where Astrology Was Born

Astrology's origins date back several thousand years. Its birthplace is believed to be the city of Babylon, the center of the flourishing southern Mesopotamia around 3500 BC. For Babylonians, the science of astrology was intertwined with religion. Moreover, during this period, astrology was still equated with astronomy, which is a completely different branch of science altogether nowadays. The mixture of eclectic concepts, Babylonian beliefs, theories, and inventions successfully laid the foundations of modern astrology. This chapter discusses what astrology meant to the Babylonians, how they used it in their day-to-day lives, and how their beliefs still affect contemporary practices.

Babylonian Astrology

The Babylonians systematically followed the stars to decipher their fate. However, unlike modern practice – where one's destiny is tied to the different planets and constellations – in Babylon, the future of someone was based on the will of the Mesopotamian deities. According to Babylonian teachings, the creator of the universe was Marduk, the god who later became the patron of the city of Babylon. It is believed that Marduk also set the Moon on its course and dictated all its phases. The rest of the planets and constellations represented other deities of the Mesopotamian pantheon who wandered the skies.

Besides having customs for honoring their deities, Babylonians also developed a tradition tied to the sky's map. They lived their lives by observing everything around them and learning from the teachings of those who lived and discovered fundamental rules before them. Their astronomers observed changes in rivers' water levels and other natural occurrences, followed by historical and economic events. As recorded in clay tablets recovered from the archaeological finds on the territory of ancient Babylon, astronomers at the time had so-called "regular watchings." They conducted these observations on the top of ziggurats, high-rising structures with an open terrace built for this exact purpose. From there, we know that for them, all earthly events were linked to the movements of the sky. They used the constellations to form a calendar for harvest and farming activities. This tradition was adopted by the Greeks and later by Western cultures.

It's important to note that the astrological roles of celestial objects did not take away their roles as deities. Their divine functions still remained, but people learned to understand why they exist and how they impacted life on Earth and thus could prepare for these effects by acting accordingly. Each movement in the sky was seen as a way for the deities to prepare people for events that would take place on Earth. Since Marduk is also a Sun deity, the actions of this god were first tied to Earth. The Babylonians understood that the Sun provides light and heat and enhances soil fertility. Hence, it's indispensable for the survival of plants, animals, and human civilization. Because of this, tracking its movements was essential during the active agricultural stages such as planting, harvesting, hunting, etc. While the Moon was initially seen as a guide during the night, tracking it soon became just as fundamental for the success of the agricultural season. The stars were seen as deities with less significant roles – and by themselves, they rarely left a measurable impression on astronomers. However, when observed as a constellation, the stars revealed many present and future events Babylonians could prepare for. The early records of Babylonian astronomers don't indicate a direct link between constellations and earthly events. However, they noted that these constellations could affect the impact of the other celestial objects. The Babylonians personified the winds, the rise of water levels, and other natural events as gods because they were seen as the actions of deities. And after the observations were made about the constellations, they started to identify stars in the same way. This was, once again, mainly due to the Babylonian astronomers' ability to combine religion, astronomy, and astrology. By applying this complex network of theories, they formed a system that provided a connection between the stars of the universe and the occurrences on Earth.

The basis for both the rustic and the divine roles of the constellation changes can be found in fundamental laws of physics and mathematical calculations used to prove them. Using these, Babylonians made precise predictions about planetary motions, despite the lack of equipment for sighting objects or calculating their movements, just as we have in modern times.

There were, however, some discrepancies between the Babylonian description of planetary systems and what modern science has since uncovered. For example, according to Babylonians, celestial bodies moved in an arc. And because their astronomers didn't understand the complex configuration of the solar system, they believed this arc to be reversible, causing the bodies to move in what's known today as retrograde motion.

After millennia of observations and learning from the variable success of their predictions, they've improved this theory by adding the Moon as another determining factor in the movements of the other celestial bodies. Although they didn't understand lunar movements, they still noted that the variability of activities increased during the new Moon phase. Nevertheless, their observations of the Moon ultimately led to the creation and the following of the lunar month - another tradition widely accepted in modern astrology. After understanding the changes in planetary velocity, they learned to predict known astrological points using the same principle modern science applies to waves. From this, Babylonians deduced that the motions of the other celestial bodies result from the Earth's movement around the Sun. Although this theory has since been disproven, it led to different hypotheses about the meaning of these events. Some of these are still applied in modern times.

Over time, the calculated mappings of the Babylonians led to the evolution of a reliable calendar that could foresee eclipses in the future and determine when they happened in the past. This allowed them to learn about the past's celestial and earthly events. Despite the complexity of the calculations needed for this and the lack of equipment on their part, Babylonians revealed issues that endangered them in the past with high accuracy, allowing future generations to avoid them.

Nowadays, we know that our brain creates images and predictions based on the stimuli generated in our optic nerve as we observe the world around us. The work of the Babylonian astronomers is, in fact, one of the earliest examples of this theory. By combining scientific observations and theoretical understanding, they enormously contributed to their thriving society. Each generation was able to leave this knowledge behind for the next generations, empowering them to achieve more and learn more about the connection between the celestial bodies and the happenings on Earth. This allowed the Babylonian civilization to develop more productive harvest, farming, and trading practices and leave behind a unique scientific legacy. The Babylonian way of observing life inspired philosophers and scientists who lived through the many centuries after their ancient civilization. Not only that, but their traditions tied together religious beliefs and the concepts of astronomy and astrology. And while, in modern times, not all three ideas are used together at all times, you'll still find at least two of them working in tandem. For example, the most accurate astrological predictions are still made by observing the movement of the different planets and constellations - just as it was done in Babylon.

Zodiac Signs

Babylonian astronomers followed and predicted that the Sun's, Moon's, and planets' positions weren't the only celestial movements. While there are no references to astrological houses in the Babylonian cuneiform inscriptions, there is clear evidence that they made observations about zodiac signs. Between 1000 BC and 500 BC, astronomers recorded the positions of the Sun, the Moon, and all the other visible celestial bodies each time they observed on top of a ziggurat.

The descriptions of the 12 zodiac signs in Babylonian astrology are derived from a combination of religious ideas and constellations observed by applying astronomical principles. Although the term "zodiac" was devised later by the Greeks, the Neo-Babylonians named the signs.

Aries is "The Hired Man"
Taurus is "The Stars"
Gemini is "The Twins"
Leo is "The Lion"
Cancer is "The Crab"
Virgo is "The Barley stalk"
Libra is "The Balance"
Pisces is "The Tails"
Sagittarius is "The Pabilsag"
Scorpio is "The Scorpion"
Capricorn is "The Goat-Fish"

The Greeks renamed the constellations as soon as they adopted them. Each zodiac sign corresponds to a constellation through which the Sun and the other planets pass over each month.

With some exceptions, the dependence of the modern astrological nomenclature on its Babylonian ancestor is undeniable – and this is even because when adopted by the Greeks, the zodiac signs only came to be seen as a combination of stars. Both modern astrology and astronomy recognize the importance of this dependence. After all, it provided the foundation for modern scientists to develop theories on the accurate stations of all the celestial bodies. Once again, developing divinatory practices is only one of the purposes of observing constellations. More and more people are discovering the usefulness of following lunar cycles for bettering their life, not to mention getting the most out of the Sun's power throughout the year.

Astrolabes

Apart from the numerous text recordings of the knowledge gathered by their scholars, Babylonians also left behind several inventions that stood as testimony to their scientific advancements. One of these inventions was the *astrolabe*, a seemingly primitive device that revolutionized science soon after its appearance. This device furthered the development of sciences, such as mathematics, physics, astronomy, and astrology. Astrolabes are essentially the almanacs of the celestial bodies. They indicate the position of planets with incredibly sharp accuracy and many other information astrologers need for navigating between and below the stars. Since Babylonians relied on astrology to predict the weather condition, astrolabes were a great help during the agricultural season. In addition to this role, astrolabes were also a reliable navigation tool. Not only do these functions were essential at the time of their invention, but they continue to inspire the makers of modern analog gadgets like mechanical watches with navigation features. Even in modern times, astrolabes can be used to determine your location and the exact time. They can also reveal your horoscope and make decisions about your future.

The original astrolabe was made from papyrus – and it consisted of a central disk (or matter) and a stack of sliding features arranged around the disk. Within the disk is a plate with a two-dimensional projection of the latitudinal lines of the Earth. Over this is a similarly shaped plate called the "rete," which illustrates the locations of celestial bodies. The linear feature above the second plate could be aligned with the time measurements on the central disk. On the back of the disk is a device designed to determine the altitudes of the start. The latter is often used as a starting point – particularly when calculating distance. Initially, Babylonians only used one plate that determined the latitude in one geographical area. As the popularity of astrolabes grew, they realized that travelers often needed to adjust to different latitudes due to the difference in geographical locations they visited on their voyages. Their solution to this problem was to produce astrolabes with latitude plates associated with the world's major cities.

MUL.APIN

Even though it contains a much shorter text than most of their written records, *MUL.APIN* is one of the most crucial astronomy texts left behind by the ancient Babylonians. The document is named after the first line of the text, as it is customary for archeological treatises from the Mesoptamina era. This first line contains the name of the constellation "The Plough," which, nowadays, you can identify by searching around the constellations of Triangulum, Cassiopeia, and Andromeda.

There are a little over 60 copies of MUL.APIN - with the oldest one dating back to around 686 BC and the youngest one dating back to approximately 300 BC. Other archaeological evidence from the same region suggests that most of the data for the oldest copies have been gathered around 1000 BC or before. Although many copies have been found in different geographical locations, there are very few variations in the 400 lines of text the document contains. The lack of discrepancies strongly contributes to the stability and reliability of this astrological compendium. There are, however, slight differences in the complexity of the texts in each list. This indicates that the data for the different lists were compiled over some time. For instance, the first list contains low-complexity texts – but as Babylonian astrologers took more and more time for observation, the complexity of the text slowly started to increase.

In two different tablets, MUL.APIN contains the name, position, and movements of the most influential celestial bodies, culmination dates, shadow measurements, weather patterns, and much more information based on the Babylonian star map. The first tablet can be a valuable tool for those wanting to reconstruct the original map because it incorporates data on the locations of various constellations with the calendar and each other. To reveal the Babylonian star map, you have six different sections at your disposal. These list the major stars and constellations allocated per three different latitudes (33, 23, and 15 stars, respectively), the attributes of the deities linked to them, and heliacal rising dates of many stars as per a 360-day calendar year. The first tablet reveals a list of constellations and stars that set and rise synchronously, the number of days between the rising of those that move asynchronously, and the list of objects that culminate around the same time. In addition, you'll find the Babylonian ancestors of the zodiac signs as part of the constellation group on the Moon's path.

Interestingly enough, the first tablet of the MUL.APIN reveals a year composed of 12 months as the ideal calendar year when Babylonians used calendars of 13 months based on the movements of the Moon and Sun. The difference between the lunisolar year and the ideal calendar year may seem difficult to grasp, but it doesn't necessarily have to be. Supposing that each month has the ideal number of 30 days makes a 12-month calendar much easier to track. In this case, every solstice would fall on the 15th of the fourth and tenth months, while the equinoxes would fall on the first and seventh months.

The second tablet of the MUL.APIN sparked an even greater interest for scientists and historians alike. It provides a comprehensive insight into the ancient wisdom of Babylonian astrology, allowing the readers to make calculations for predicting the movements of the Sun, Moon, and planets. It also provides the unique ability to trace back these events and explore them in the past. It contains the names of all the celestial bodies that travel on the same path as the Moon. From it, you can learn which solstices and equinoxes fall under the full Moon and familiarize yourself with lunar and solar cycles in general. You can see the duration of the nights and days during the major festivities and a mathematical scheme to calculate the rising of the Moon for each month. The tablet also enumerates the stars linked to the four directional winds and the date when the Sun is located in one of the three stellar paths described on the first tablet. There is an approximate date on which each planet is visible – and some recommendations on using all the previously mentioned in the text.

Last but not least, this tablet also reveals a list of astrological omens. Since omens played a fundamental part in the Mesopotamian belief systems, they were said to be messages coming directly from their deities. Babylonians placed heavy emphasis on staying in favor of the gods. They created the omens to engage with their gods and to communicate with them. They used omens during rituals and offerings or as a celestial tie to another planet. Planets are gods' physical and astrological representation, meaning they have a significant part in causing omens to appear. Understanding how omens work and how to decipher them can serve as divination tools even in modern times. This particularly applies if you seek specific information about future astrological events. However, as the information on this list seems incomplete, this may imply the existence of a third tablet - one that has yet to be found. There are two different formats for the omens listed on this tablet. One indicates the occurrence, while the other implies the appearance of omens. The first one suggests that an omen can occur anytime. Whereas the latter means that the omen will appear at a specific time.

Chapter 4: Egyptian Astrology and the Decans

No one can deny the impact ancient Egyptians have on various fields like mathematics, writing, architecture, medicine, and astrology. They weren't just interested or fascinated with astrology. It played a major role in their everyday life as well. They believed their deities appeared to them in various forms, and each of their gods and goddesses was associated with a star or a planet. According to ancient Egyptian mythology, Thoth, the god of the moon, writing, and learning (Hermes in Greek mythology), taught various subjects, including astrology, to his priests and disciples. He also believed that he wrote four books about astrology and carved magical teachings about heavenly bodies on temple walls.

The ancient Egyptians believed that whatever happens in the cosmos can influence each person's life and result in environmental changes. For this reason, temple priests paid a lot of attention to astrology by observing the stars, their movements, and their positions. They designed their temples to help them monitor the stars by incorporating arch ceilings in the temples so they would look like the heavens. For their rituals, the temple priests would only schedule and perform them during planetary activities.

During ancient times, astrology was still relatively new, so there was no such thing as an astrologer. The ancient Egyptians believed astrology was divine, so temple priests were the only ones who acted as astrologers back then. They recorded all the information they gathered from monitoring the stars to understand better how the cosmos can affect someone's personality and mood. The ancient Egyptians were inspired by how the Greeks designated their zodiac signs and decided to do the same by applying it to their gods.

Ancient Egyptians put so much stock in astrology and believed the movements of the stars could help them predict disasters like floods and famine; they even used it to determine the best time to plant their crops. Unlike how people nowadays use astrology, ancient Egyptians took it very seriously. They considered it to be sacred and that it was given to them by the gods. Astrology wasn't just used for predictions; it was used in various areas of their lives as well. For instance, astrology played a huge role in medicine and helped treat people with various diseases.

The ancient Egyptians used a calendar as well. The Gregorian calendar we use now is quite similar to the ancient Egyptian calendar, as they are both considered solar calendars. That said, there are some differences. Both calendars have 365 days a year; however, there are only three seasons a year, with each season consisting of 120 days. You have probably noticed that there are still five days left in the year. The ancient Egyptians added an extra month for these five days, but this month wasn't considered a part of the year. There were also 12 months, like in the Gregorian calendar, named after their main festivals or numbered within each season.

Weeks were also different in the ancient Egyptian calendar; each week was ten days instead of seven, with only three weeks a month. The ten-day week was called "decan," and there were 36 decans a year. The last two days of every decan (week) were like a weekend when royal craftsmen took time off.

Ancient Egyptian Astrology vs. Babylonian Astrology

As mentioned, Babylonians are believed to be the ones who invented astrology, so it makes sense that they heavily influenced the ancient Egyptians. The Babylonian culture influenced ancient Egyptian astrology in various ways. For starters, to calculate

Mercury's position in the sky, the ancient Egyptians used Babylonian methods. Around 330 B.C, Egypt was conquered by Alexander the Great, who then created the city of Alexandria, which is still standing today. Alexandria was the birthplace of the Egyptian zodiac signs by integrating Decanic astrology with the Greek Babylonian astrology.

However, the ancient Egyptians managed to stand out from the Babylonians by creating the "decans," which played a huge role in dividing the day into 24 hours as opposed to the Babylonians, who divided it into 12 hours. Both cultures managed to stand out with original and unique creations. The Babylonians were the ones who created the calendar, while the ancient Egyptians created the "decan" and later applied it to the zodiac.

By dividing the stars into constellations and creating what is now known as zodiac signs, the Babylonians influenced many cultures like the Greeks and ancient Egyptians.

Ancient Egypt and Modern Astrology

Ancient Egyptians have influenced modern astrology because they were one of the first civilizations to divide the year into 365 days and the day into 24 hours. Zodiac signs were different in Egypt as they had no interest in the 12 constellations developed by the Greeks. Instead, they opted for the "decans" and divided the constellation into 36 small groups. This made their zodiac signs quite different from the ones we use nowadays. In the coming chapters, we will discuss the ancient Egyptian zodiac signs in detail.

Decans

We have mentioned "decans" a few times in this chapter, and now you are probably left with one question, what are decans? As you know, zodiac signs are divided into 12 constellations, each including various characteristics for people who share the same signs. However, do all people who share the same sign have the exact same qualities? If you look at the characteristics and traits of your sign, you'll probably find a couple or more that don't apply to you. You may have met people born under your zodiac sign but share nothing in common with you. Decans answer the question of why two people born under the same zodiac sign don't necessarily share the same personality traits, hobbies, likes, dislikes, or habits.

Decans subdivide each zodiac sign without impacting any of the signs' personality traits. It helps shed light on different factors of a sign. Each zodiac sign has three decans dividing it into ten-degree increments to help break down their personality traits. Just like a planet rules each zodiac sign, each decan also has a planetary ruler who acts as a sub-ruler to the zodiac sign. Each sub-ruler planet will provide unique qualities for each decan to help you learn more about yourself. In other words, zodiac signs give more of a general idea while decans narrow down qualities with the help of sub-rulers planets, so they are more specific to people born in the first, second, or last ten days of a sign. However, people born on the first ten days of any sign will usually embody the sign's qualities and personality traits because their sub-ruler planet and the sign's ruler planet are the same.

This doesn't affect the sign you were born into at all. For instance, if you are a Libra, you'll still be a Libra – you will just have a decan to help you better understand your personality.

The decans were created by the ancient Egyptians; this invention made Egyptian astrology stand out from other civilizations. The Greeks were inspired by them and created their own decan; they called it "decanoi," which means *ten days apart*.

To learn about your decan, you should first find your degree. Each person has their own unique degree, and you can find it in your birth chart. However, you can figure your decan out by yourself. Each sign lasts for approximately 30 days, with the first representing the first ten days. The second and third are for the next ten and the ten after, respectively.

Decans should have the same element as the sign they are assigned to. For instance, an air sign should only have air decans, not water, fire, or earth. Decans are also arranged in order, i.e., the first decan is applied to the first ten degrees of a sign, the second to the second ten, and so on. When you understand decans, it will finally make sense why two people born under the same sign have different characteristics; they may even be opposites since each has a different decan.

As mentioned, if you are born in the first ten days, it will be easy to find your decan because your sub-planet ruler is the same as your sign's ruler. However, suppose you are born in the second or third decan. In that case, you can follow the Chaldean Order or the Elemental Triplicities, considered a more modern method.

The Chaldean Order

The Chaldean Order is believed to be the first and oldest method created to help people find their decans. This method only uses the five wandering stars and two lights, the Sun and the Moon. Each zodiac sign is assigned three planets (one for each decan). They are usually arranged based on their Chaldean Order, which is from slowest to fastest, and each planet serves as a first, second, and third decan.

- **Aries:** Mars, Sun, and Venus
- **Taurus:** Mercury, the Moon, and Saturn
- **Gemini:** Jupiter, Mars, and the Sun
- **Cancer:** Venus, Mercury, and the Moon
- **Leo:** Saturn, Jupiter, and Mars
- **Virgo:** Sun, Venus, and Mercury
- **Libra:** The Moon, Saturn, and Jupiter
- **Scorpio:** Mars, Sun, and Venus
- **Sagittarius:** Mercury, the Moon, and Saturn
- **Capricorn:** Jupiter, Mars, and the Sun
- **Aquarius:** Venus, Mercury, and the Moon
- **Pisces:** Saturn, Jupiter, and Mars

The Elemental Triplicities

The Elemental Triplicities is a modern way to help you find out your decan—. It divides zodiac signs into threes based on their elements: air, fire, water, and earth. This method is quite different from the Chaldean Order. As mentioned, the first decan has the same sub-ruler planet as the sign's ruler planet. You can then move on to the second and third decans and the associated element positions. This may sound confusing, but it is much simpler than you think.

To help you better understand how this works, take a look at each sign, its element, and its ruling planet.

Air Signs
- Gemini ruled by Mercury
- Libra ruled by Venus
- Aquarius ruled by Uranus

Fire Signs
- Aries ruled by Mars
- Leo ruled by the sun
- Sagittarius ruled by Jupiter

Water Signs
- Cancer ruled by the moon
- Scorpio ruled by Pluto
- Pisces, ruled by Neptune

Earth Signs
- Taurus ruled by Venus
- Virgo ruled by Mercury
- Capricorn ruled by Saturn

To make things clearer, if you are born under Gemini and want to figure out your decan, the first days of the sign are ruled by Mercury, the sub-ruler. The second 10 days will have Venus as its decan since Libra is the second planet in this triplicity, while the last ten days will have Uranus as the decan since Aquarius is the third sign in the element.

This method is very popular in the West and has been used since the 20th century. However, Indian astrologers have been using it way before then.

Decans have proven to survive the test of time as astrologers and individuals prefer using them to understand their weaknesses, strengths, and potential. You can also learn about your decan to understand the different layers of your personality. If the methods mentioned here seem complicated, especially if you are a beginner, we will also help you find your decan and some of its personality traits.

Find Your Decan

Aries (March 21st to April 19th)

- The first decan falls from March 21st to March 30th. It is an Aries decan and ruled by Mars. People born under the first decan are considered "pure Aries" who embody the sign's characteristics and its ruler planet. They are energetic, passionate, ambitious, competitive, independent, adventurous, and confident people with child-like innocence.
- The second decan is from March 30th to April 9th. It is a Leo decan with the Sun as its sub-ruler. People born under this decan live by their principles and are very noble. They are strong-willed, focused, and stick to their goals and ambitions no matter what. However, with Leo's ego and the self-righteousness of the Aries, people born under this decan can appear smug.
- The third decan is from April 10 to April 19. This is a Sagittarius decan with Jupiter as its sub-ruler. They are independent, intellectual, open, optimistic, and individuals.

Taurus (20th April to 20th May)

- The first decan is from April 20th to April 29th. This is a Taurus decan ruled by Venus. These individuals love living in luxury and enjoy beautiful things that engage their five senses. They are also stable, determined, and peacemakers.
- The second decan is from April 30th to May 9th. This is a Virgo decan with Mercury as its sub-ruler. These people are incredibly charming and can be mesmerizing with their speech and tone of voice. They are more graceful than people born under the first decan and can be a bit shy.
- The third decan is from May 10th to May 19th. This is a Capricorn decan with Saturn as its sub-ruler. They are steady, loyal, and have a great sense of humor. They are extremely disciplined and may seem serious until you get to know them.

Gemini (21st May to 20th June)
- The first decan is from May 22nd to May 31st. It is a Gemini decan ruled by Mercury. They are curious, intelligent, social, quick-witted, and always up for interesting conversations.
- The second decan is from June 1st to June 10. This is a Libra decan with the Moon as its sub-ruler. They are lovers of beauty, enjoy deep conversations, and are very sensual.
- The third decan is from June 11th to June 21st. This is an Aquarius decan with Uranus as its sub-ruler. They are rebellious, independent, friendly, and sociable.

Cancer (21st June to 22nd July)
- The first decan is from June 22nd to July 1st. This is a Cancer decan ruled by the moon. Individuals under this decan are nurturing, sensitive, compassionate, energetic, and caring but can be very jealous.
- The second decan is from July 2nd to July 12th. This is a Scorpio decan with Pluto as its ruler. They are giving and have great instincts, making them excel as therapists or detectives.
- The third decan is from July 13th to July 22nd. This is a Pisces decan with Neptune as its sub-ruler. They are extremely sensitive individuals who put others' needs before their own.

Leo (23rd July to 22nd August)
- The first decan is from July 23rd to August 1st. This is a Leo decan, and it is ruled by the Sun. People born under this decan are independent, warm, and energetic but tend to seek others' approval.
- The second decan is from August 2nd to August 11tth. This is a Sagittarius decan with Jupiter as its sub-ruler. They are risk-takers, adventurous, and more fun than a typical Leo.
- The third decan is from August 12th to August 22nd. This is an Aries decan with Mars as its sub-ruler. They are ambitious, honest, optimistic, and kind-hearted but can be

extremely stubborn.

Virgo (23rd August to 22nd September)

- The first decan is from August 23rd to September 1st. This is a Virgo decan ruled by Mercury. These individuals are punctual, organized, and detail-oriented.
- The second decan is from September 2nd to September 11th. This is a Capricorn decan with Saturn as its sun-ruler. They are responsible, determined, hard-working, good with money, and ambitious but lack flexibility.
- The third decan is from from September 12th to September 22nd. This is a Taurus decan with Venus as its sub-ruler. They are reserved, steady, and quiet and have an impeccable sense of style.

Libra (23rd September to 22nd October)

- The first decan is from September 23rd to October 2nd. This is a Libra decan ruled by Venus; they are extremely romantic and enjoy the finer things in life.
- The second decan is from October 4th to October 12th. This is an Aquarius decan with Uranus as its sub-ruler. They are inventive and social, and they care about other people.
- The third decan is from October 13th to October 22nd. This is a Gemini decan with Mercury as its sub-ruler. They have great communication skills and are considered social, intuitive, and extremely charming.

Scorpio (23rd October to 21st November)

- The first decan is from October 23rd to November 1st. This is a Scorpio decan ruled by Pluto. These people are passionate, intense, seductive, and calculating.
- The second decan is from November 2nd to November 11th. This is a Pisces decan with Neptune as its sub-ruler. They are mysterious, authentic, and creative with great imagination.
- The third decan is from November 12th to November 21st. This is a Cancer decan with the moon as its sub-ruler.

These people are sensitive caretakers, and they rarely compromise.

Sagittarius (22nd November to 21st December)

- The first decan is from November 22nd to December 1st. This is a Sagittarius decan, and it is ruled by Jupiter. They are free-spirited, optimistic, adventurous, and non-conformists.
- The second decan is from December 2nd to December 11th. This is an Aries decan with Mars as its sub-ruler. They are confident, brave, headstrong, and always looking for a new challenge.
- The third decan is from December 12th to December 21st. This is a Leo decan with the Sun as its sun-ruler. These people are charismatic and energetic but can be quite impulsive.

Capricorn (22nd December to 19th January)

- The first decan is from December 2nd to December 31st. This is a Capricorn decan ruled by Saturn. They are ambitious, confident, practical, realistic, and disciplined with a great sense of humor.
- The second decan is from January 1st to January 10th. This is a Taurus decan with Venus as its sub-ruler. They are romantic, sensual, hard-working, and enjoy the finer things in life.
- The third decan is from January 11th to January 19th. This is a Virgo decan with Mercury as its sun-ruler. They are ambitious, organized, and intelligent.

Aquarius (20th January to 18th February)

- The first decan is from January 20th to January 29th. This is an Aquarius decan and ruled by Uranus. They are insightful, reasonable, freethinkers, and non-conformists.
- The second decan is from January 30th to February 8th. This is a Gemini decan with Mercury as its sub-ruler. They are chatty, bright, and intellectuals.

- The third decan is from February 9th to February 18th. This is a Libra decan with Venus as its sub-ruler. They are graceful, sociable, and likable. They are interested in all pleasures life has to offer, especially romance.

Pisces (19th February to 20th March)

- The first decan is from February 19th to February 28th. This is a Pisces decan and ruled by Neptune. These people are intuitive, creative, and the least egotistical people you'll ever meet.

- The second decan is from March 1st to March 10th. This is a Cancer decan ruled by the Moon. They are extremely sensitive, sweet, and loyal.

- The third decan is from March 11th to March 20th. This is a Scorpio decan with Pluto as its sub-ruler. These people are calculating, mysterious, spiritual, and can be prone to jealousy.

As it is obvious from the invention of decans, the ancient Egyptians contributed so much to the world of astrology. The ancient Egyptians also divided the day into 24 hours and the year into 365 days. However, their contributions don't end here. There are also the ancient Egyptian astrological signs which we will discuss in the next chapter.

Chapter 5: The Egyptian Zodiac Signs

We have discussed in the previous chapters how priests served as astrologers by monitoring the star's movements. However, when scientists compared early ancient Egyptian findings and predictions with those of later dynastic periods (when ancient Greece heavily influenced Egypt), they found a huge difference between the two which sparked a heated debate among scientists.

Ancient Egyptian's zodiac signs are a very hot topic among historians as some believe the ancient Egyptians created their own version of a horoscope, while others believe there is nothing to prove they had any interest in zodiac constellations. However, when the Greek civilization dominated ancient Egyptians, evidence of zodiac signs and constellations was discovered later in history.

The ancient Egyptian zodiac.
Inigo. Barlow; Thomas Maurice (1754-1824); F Wilford Attribution 4.0 International (CC BY 4.0) < https://creativecommons.org/licenses/by/4.0/>
https://www.lookandlearn.com/history-images/YW024914V/Astronomy-the-twelve-signs-of-the-zodiac

Ancient Egyptians Zodiac Signs

Although Western zodiac signs are very popular, they aren't the only ones out there. Other ancient cultures worldwide have created their own zodiac signs, including the ancient Egyptians. Like the

Western zodiac, the Ancient Egyptians also created 12 signs named after one of their deities. However, only one zodiac sign is named after their famous river, the Nile. It was believed the character of the deity the sign is named after embodies the characteristics of the person born under it. The ancient Egyptians used zodiac signs the same way we use them today to help them learn about their personality traits. However, unlike Western zodiac signs, the Egyptians didn't assign a month for each sign; instead, they assigned specific days.

Now, let's take a look at each of the 12 zodiac signs so you can learn more about yourself from your Egyptian zodiac sign.

The Nile (1-7 January, 19-28 June, 1-7 September, 18-26 November)

Western Sign

Capricorn

Positive and Negative Traits

- Peaceful
- Practical
- Logical
- Insightful
- Wise
- Domineering
- Impulsive

Ruling Planets

Uranus and the Moon

Animal

The Antelope

God

This is the only sign not named after a god. The Nile is an important body of water to Egyptians. They held the river in high regard and considered it the source of life and vital for their survival. Some Egyptians considered it a deity, worshiped it, and prayed to it when they needed something. Today, modern

Egyptians still consider the Nile their source of life.

Most Compatible With

Set and Amun-Ra

Personality Traits

People born under this sign are known to be very passionate and peaceful. They hate nothing more than missing an opportunity and would rather act now than regret it later. They dislike conflict and can make others feel calm and at peace whenever they are around them. They are considered very wise individuals, very intelligent, and have strong observation and communication skills. Making friends comes easily to this sign because of their helpful, selfless, and giving personality. They love the finer things in life and hope one day to become wealthy. These people are also practical, cautious, and patient. They are extremely adaptable, which makes them suitable for various professions.

On the other hand, people born under the Nile sign can be impulsive and prone to having emotional outbursts every now and then. They are usually obsessed with details, making them nervous and disturbing their inner peace. They can be a bit moody and go from being quiet and calm to angry and irrational.

Amon-Ra (8-21 January, 1-11 February)

Western Sign

Taurus

Positive and Negative Traits

- Helpful
- Generous
- Powerful
- Successful
- Secretive

Ruling Planets

Saturn and the Sun

Animal

The Ram

God
Amun-Ra is the king of all gods; he created the universe and all of mankind. It is believed that he gave people the ability to create things from nothing.

Most Compatible With
Horus and the Nile

Personality Traits
People born under this sign are optimistic and talented. Leadership comes naturally to them because they are trustworthy. They are highly intuitive; a quality they use to fix any problem they face. They would never say no to anyone asking for help since they are giving people who are happy to lend a helping hand. They are strong leaders, very confident, and remain in control no matter what happens around them. They are very classy; you may even mistake them for royalty. Some of the happiest people you'll ever meet are born under this sign; you'll find them always optimistic with a smile on their faces. They are very lucky individuals who always find success. They are perfect for jobs like motivational speakers, counselors, or life coaches because others find them inspiring and go to them for advice. Great listeners, intelligence, and good decision-makers are all the qualities that make them suitable for leadership positions like managers or CEOs.

On the other hand, they are so focused on their career and helping others that they may neglect their home life. For this reason, they may not be inclined to start a family. Stubborn with a huge ego, there is no going back once they decide. They won't listen to anyone's advice because they can be unyielding.

Mut (22-31 January, 8-22 September)

Western Sign
Scorpio

Positive and Negative Traits
- Hardworking
- Attentive
- Ironic

- Unfriendly
- Cranky

Ruling Planet
The Sun

Animal
Vulture

God
Mut is a female deity. She is the goddess of the sky and is considered the mother of all mankind and the one responsible for protecting them.

Most Compatible With
Thoth and Amun-Ra

Personality Traits
Since Mut is a mother goddess, individuals born under this sign are known to be nurturing and very protective of the people in their lives. However, they also need to feel protected and are always looking for someone who can act as a parent and look out for them. As a result of their nurturing nature, they can also be great parents and role models. They only open up to those closest to them and keep their thoughts and feelings hidden from everyone else. They are very shy by nature, especially in new relationships, but once you get to know them, you'll see how generous and wise they are. Serious and committed in relationships, they can be great partners. They are goal-oriented and know exactly what they want out of life. Focused and determined, they will do whatever it takes to achieve their goals. People are usually attracted to them because they are charming and good listeners.

When it comes to their negative traits, people born under the Mut sign can be too involved in their relationships. Since they are very committed, they usually expect their relationship to last, and when it doesn't, they become very disappointed. They are prone to long episodes of depression and sadness. In relationships, they often seem cold and rarely show their feelings, mostly because they are secretive individuals. They often think that showing affection will make them seem vulnerable or weak. They have explosive tempers and would rather give the silent treatment than talk things out. Mut individuals often criticize others but don't handle criticism very well.

Geb (February 12-29 and August 20-31)

Western Sign
Libra

Positive and Negative Traits
- Fair
- Modest
- Proud
- Sensitive
- Affectionate
- Anxious
- Vain

Ruling Planet
Earth

Animal
Goose

God
Geb is the god of the earth. It is believed that his laughter could cause earthquakes. He plays a huge role in the afterlife as he is one of the gods that weigh the deceased people's hearts to determine their fate.

Most Compatible With
Set and Horus

Personality Traits
Sensitive and kind-hearted, people born under this sign are usually very attentive to other people's feelings. They are highly intuitive and compassionate, making them seem very emotional. They are introverted individuals who always listen to their gut feeling. They can be very empathetic and are deeply affected by anything that happens in the world. As a result, they may avoid watching the news or going on social media to protect themselves from all the negativity in the world. If you ask your Geb friend for a favor, rest assured they will come through for you because they are

very reliable individuals. Although they are highly sensitive, they manage to keep their feelings under control and remain composed during any situation. They aren't impulsive; they think before acting. They can be shy at times, but, when necessary, they can also be assertive. They are always there for other people and would never forget it if you lent them a helping hand. Careers like writing, counseling, or teaching are perfect for them. Just like their counterpart Libra, they love the finer things in life and are lovers of beauty.

As a result of their kind nature, people often can take advantage of individuals born under the Geb sign. At times, they can be vain and suffer from huge egos. They don't know how to set healthy boundaries and say no to others because they don't want to hurt anyone's feelings.

Osiris (March 1-10, November 27- December 18)

Western Sign

Aries

Positive and Negative Traits

- Bold
- Energetic
- Domineering
- Bossy
- Indecisive

Ruling Planets

The Sun and Pluto

Animal

Bull

God

Osiris is the god of the dead and the afterlife. He symbolizes fertility, resurrection, and rebirth.

Most Compatible With

Isis and Thoth

Personality Traits

Having a dual personality is an accurate description of this sign. They can either be strong and feisty or vulnerable and indecisive. You'll find that they get excited about the New Year because they love new beginnings and are hopeful about their future. They are innovative and suitable for careers like teaching or sales. People born under this sign can be perfect for leadership positions because they're intelligent and charismatic individuals. For sure, leadership comes easily to them because they are confident and goal-oriented. They are also flexible, can easily cope with change, and are determined individuals who would never let anything stand between them and their dreams. They are direct, energetic, and live in the moment. They are also confident, adventurous, and fiercely independent.

However, they don't like taking orders from other people, even if it is their boss. They may show an aggressive or dominating attitude to anyone above them. Arguing with them can be exhausting because of their huge ego, which can impact their relationships. With the smallest misunderstanding, they may lose their temper and explode. As a result, working with them can be very difficult. They are good leaders but don't know how to follow and can't handle criticism.

Isis (11-31 March, 18-29 October, 19-31 December)

Western Sign

Pisces

Positives and Negatives

- Passionate
- Ambitious
- Dignified
- Straightforward
- Hyperactive
- Demanding

Ruling Planets
Earth, Uranus, and the Moon
Animal
Ram
God
Isis is another female deity. She is the goddess of nature and the protector of children, the poor, and the dead. She is also a mother's guardian as she protects them when they are giving birth.
Most Compatible With
Osiris and Thoth
Personality Traits
You'll never experience any misunderstandings with these individuals by seeing how they are straightforward. They love being in love and always have faith in their relationships. They prefer partners who are carefree and adventurous. They are energetic and have great communication skills and a playful attitude. People are usually attracted to them because of their great sense of humor. They are very protective of the people in their lives and always ready to put a smile on their faces. They are suitable for careers that involve rational thinking and disciplining others like supervisors or leaders.

On the other hand, they can be too demanding, which can strain their relationships. They get bored and restless and often crave change. As a result, they may struggle to focus on their goals and will keep finding new ones and switching between them. This can distract them from achieving anything. Serious is a word they aren't very fond of, and they avoid serious situations like the plague.

Thoth (April 1 – 19, November 8 – 17)
Western Sign
Virgo
Positive and Negative Traits
- Great listeners
- Possess leadership skills
- Compassionate

- Courageous
- Energetic
- Difficult to work with
- Naive

Ruling Planets

Mercury and the Moon

Animal

Baboon

God

Thoth is the god of wisdom and learning. He created writing and is considered the record keeper of everything.

Most Compatible With

Isis and Bastet

Personality Traits

If you are looking for a problem solver, people born under this sign are the ones to look for. They are creative and enjoy sharing the things they have learned. This can make them suitable for a teaching career. They are very organized and have high communication skills. Since the god of writing rules them, they can make great journalists or writers. They are very loyal in romantic relationships and look for stable partners who value family, just like them.

They can be impatient and make impulsive decisions. Naive and too trusting, these individuals only see the good in people, leading them to disappointment when they are wrong. They can sometimes be stubborn and unable to see things from others' points of view.

Horus (April 20-May 7, August 12-19)

Western Sign

Aquarius

Positive and Negative Traits

- Charming
- Wit
- Endurance

- Strong-willed
- Inflexible
- Stubborn

Ruling Planets
The Sun and the Moon

Animal
Snake

God
Horus is one of the most popular ancient Egyptian gods. He is the god of the sky and the protector of the pharaohs. It is believed he was the one that united Upper and Lower Egypt.

Most Compatible With
Geb and Bastet

Personality Traits
Unafraid to take risks, people born under this sign are very courageous. They enjoy trying new things and would never say no to any opportunity. They are very charismatic and optimistic individuals. As a result of their courage, they can excel in any career they choose. Inspiring, motivated, and natural leaders know what they want and aren't afraid to go after it. They are strong-willed, ambitious, and very devoted to their families, putting them first. They are selfless, great listeners, and kind. People born under this sign can help you solve any problem you face. They will excel as psychologists or guidance counselors.

Unyielding, people born under a Horus sign are stubborn and inflexible in their opinions. People may see them as domineering because they enjoy being in charge. They may struggle with their relationships because of their angry outbursts and aggression.

Anubis (May 8-27, June 29-July 13)

Western Sign
Leo

Positive and Negative Qualities
- Sympathetic

- Honest
- Intelligent
- Cunning
- Competitive
- Controlling

Ruling Planet

Mercury

Animal

Jackal

God

Anubis is the god of mummification, death, and the afterlife. He also guards the underworld. He can find those who are lost to life, and he will weigh their hearts to determine if they are worthy of passing on.

Most Compatible With

Isis and Bastet

Personality Traits

Creative, passionate, sensitive, and emotional are some of the qualities people born under Anubis are famous for. They don't prefer to work in teams; they shine when they work alone. They aren't fond of crowds because of their introverted nature. However, when they are around people, they are always confident. They are extremely blunt and aren't afraid to speak their mind. Their curiosity about people, their thoughts, and how their minds work makes them suitable for careers in psychology or teaching. They can also excel in roles that involve helping others, like a doctor or a nurse. Determined, they would never give up until they achieved their goals. Being ruled by Horus, they may have a slight interest in death.

Individuals born under this sign may experience severe mood swings, they can be happy, and suddenly, they are depressed or angry. This can result from their empathetic nature and absorbing other people's emotions. They can be controlling and too competitive and would struggle if someone else was taking the lead. In relationships, they can be possessive.

Seth (May 28-June 18, September 28-October 2)

Western Sign

Gemini

Positive and Negative Traits

- Determined
- Perfectionist
- Persistent
- Impulsive
- Bad-tempered

Ruling Planet

Mars

Animal

Tiger

God

Seth is the god of chaos, earthquakes, and storms. It is believed that he could control the weather. According to an ancient legend, Seth killed his brother Osiris, chopped his body into pieces, and left each body apart in a different place in Egypt. He believed that he did that because he discovered that his wife, Nephtys, had a child with Osiris. This child is the god Anubis.

Most Compatible With

The Nile and Geb

Personality Traits

Adventurous and perfectionist, nothing can stop people born under this sign from going after what they want. They have great leadership skills and can always rise to the challenge. They don't think about the past; they learn from their mistakes and happily move on to better things in their future. Charming, charismatic, and outgoing are some of the qualities that attract people to them. They are social and love being around other people. They don't like sitting still or being idle; they always want to be busy. Their ideal job is teaching.

Bastet individuals are moody and have a very bad temper. They value their freedom and hate rules and restrictions, so they may struggle with being micromanaged or following guidelines. They have a rebellious spirit and find it hard to conform.

Bastet (14-28 July, 23-27 September, 3-17 October)

Western Sign

Cancer

Positive and Negative Traits

- Thoughtful
- Charming
- Anxious
- Clingy
- Possessive

Ruling Planets

The Sun and the Moon

Animal

Cat

God

Bastet is another female deity. She is usually called the cat goddess because she has a cat head and a human body. She is the goddess of homelife and womanhood. A guardian of women, Bastet helps them with their fertility.

Most Compatible With

Horus and Sekhmet

Personality Traits

Nothing is more important for the Bastet people than peace. They are introverts who love peace and quiet and usually avoid crowds, stressful situations, and confrontations. They are extremely intuitive; you may mistake them for psychics. They are charming individuals who live their lives to the fullest. Happiness is their number one goal which is why they surround themselves with things they find pleasing. Fiercely loyal, they are devoted to their loved ones and will always put them first. They are nurturing, sensitive, and emotional and will always protect the people in their lives. The ideal job for them is writing.

In relationships, they can be overprotective, clingy, and possessive. Trust doesn't come easy to them and is usually very secretive. They often remain hung up on past relationships for a long time and struggle to let go and move on.

Sekhmet (July 29-August 11, October 30-November 7)

Western Sign
Sagittarius

Positive and Negative Traits
- Approachable
- Cheerful
- Optimistic
- Clever
- Leadership skills
- Easily offended
- Impatient

Ruling Planet
The Sun

Animal
Lion

God
Sekhmet is the last female deity we have on this list. She is referred to as the Eye of Ra. Sekhmet, the goddess of war and a healer, ensures justice is served as she has the power to decide who is guilty and who is innocent. She has the head of a lion and the body of a woman.

Most Compatible With
Baster and Geb

Personality Traits

Like people born under Osiris, individuals born under Sekhmet have dual personalities. They can be strict and disciplined on one side; on the other, they are flexible and free. They are perfectionists, just, and have strong values. They are suitable for jobs like CEOs or judges. Professional, trustworthy, approachable, disciplined, and graceful are some of the qualities that make people respect them and feel drawn to them. Down to earth and intelligent, they find success in whatever they do. The glass is always half full of Sekhmet people. They have a sunny attitude and charming personalities.

Sekhmet individuals tend to have short tempers. They can be impatient, aggressive, and rude. They can be very focused on materialistic pursuits and can suffer from addictions. In relationships, they can be very possessive. They begin bragging about their accomplishments whenever they feel confident and make others feel inferior.

The Egyptian zodiac signs are very interesting and can help you learn about different aspects of your personality. You should definitely read more about the god of your zodiac sign because all ancient Egyptian goods have interesting legends associated with them.

Chapter 6: Hellenistic Astrology
I. The Topoi

Astrology has played a major role in almost every single civilization. However, this field of study's role in the Late-Hellenistic era is noteworthy, particularly because it blends aspects of Greek philosophy and views on an individual's dynamics of life. While horoscopic or natal charts, which divide the sky into regions describing the planetary positions, originated in Babylon, they were essentially developed in Hellenized, Greek-speaking areas. The oldest natal chart dates back to 410 BCE in Babylon. Although the incredible Babylonian advancement can't be understated, Mesopotamians had already used star omens for divination and astral spirituality for years at that point in history.

They used stars to symbolize gods they could pray to and receive favors from. You may have already heard of Anu, Enlil, and Ea, the astrological deities that are represented not only by single stars but also by constellations. The concept of planetary gods can also be found in Hellenistic astrology. Mars or Nergal was believed to be the deity of destruction and plagues, while Venus or Ištar was considered the goddess of love. A limited number of Babylonian records pertain to laconic predictions and planetary placements, making it particularly challenging to draw solid inferences regarding the conceptual basis of early horoscopic practices.

The Hellenistic Era and Modern-Day Astrology

The Hellenistic era is unique, combining numerous philosophies, including Babylonian, Egyptian, Jewish, and Persian spiritual beliefs and ideologies. Astronomy and astrology practices were already spreading in the lands of Babylon before the conquest of Alexander the Great. At that point, Greek thinkers weren't yet concerned with these areas of study. While Greece was responsible for making astrology studies popular, the Babylonian writer, Berossus, and other Babylonian astrologers and priests introduced the Greeks to the science.

Alexandria, Egypt's intellectual hub, is believed to be the home of notable Hellenistic astrology developments. Numerous Hellenistic astrologers credited the pharaoh Nechepso, who was an Egyptian priest, with the earliest and most significant astrological advancements. Hermes, the Greek god of astrology, is believed to be the inventor of astrology. Some developments that trace back to the deity's name still survive, while other authors speak of other works belonging to Nechepso. The Greek Asclepius, Pythagoras, Orpheus, the Egyptian Anubis, the Iranian Zoroaster, and the prophet Abraham are also examples of other figures associated with astrology. Late Hellenistic texts refer to Kidinnu, Sudines, Naburianos, Babylonian astronomers, and astrologers.

The source of Hellenistic astrology, and whether it can be attributed to the Egyptians or the Babylonians, is perhaps the result of Ptolemaic and Seleucid rivalries. The Babylonians and the Egyptians are primarily credited with numerous astrological charts, tables, and techniques. However, modern research suggests that some astrological methods and approaches were inaccurately traced. Egyptian calendars, spiritual practices, and religious beliefs were merged with Babylonian astrological techniques, joined by Pythagorean mathematics, Stoic and Platonist philosophies, and Hermeticism. This created a more complex and intricate astrological system that is close to what we have today.

This chapter illustrates the importance of the diurnal and nocturnal horoscopes for Greek astrologers. Then, you'll understand the word topos (places) used by Greek astrologers in more depth. Here, you'll find out what these places show, how they're calculated, and which astrological houses they're associated with. In this chapter, you'll find the meaning of each place, as well as the similarities and differences they have with their correspondent houses.

Sect: Diurnal and Nocturnal Horoscopes

The concept of "sect" is very popular in classical astrology, where the seven main planets are divided into two groups. The idea behind the sect is to identify a planet's strengths and benefic attributes in one's birth chart. Although this simple act of grouping was incredibly helpful, it was widely abandoned during the medieval age. The only reason why we hear of this practice today is that recent translation works have restored it.

Sect is originally known as $αἵρεσις$, or hairesis, in Greek. This word was used to describe opposing political or religious factions at the time. For instance, two people who belonged to different heretical groups would be known to be members of different hairesis. Astrologers in Greece ascertained that the planets could be split in two—the day and the night (diurnal and nocturnal) daytime.

Saturn, Jupiter, and the sun all belong to the day, while Venus, Mars, and the Moon belong to the night. Mercury can be part of both and move back and forth. At times, it is a morning star, rising before the sun does. At other times, it rises much later.

Just like two political parties can't be in power at the same time, only one astrological sect can dominate at a single time. As you can probably tell, the diurnal sect steps into its power as soon as the sun crosses the horizon, marking the start of daytime. The nocturnal sect is in power when it's nighttime, and the Sun rests below the horizon. People born in the daytime have a daytime chart where the Sun is in power, and those born at night have a nighttime chart.

Suppose you want to know whether the diurnal or the nocturnal sect rules your chart. In that case, you have to determine the location of the Sun in relevance to the horizon at the time of your birth. If the Sun lies in houses 2 through 6, you have a nighttime chart at the bottom of the chart. The Sun lies in houses 12 through 8, indicating a daytime chart. If the Sun is located at either the 1st or 7th house with whole sign houses, you need to check where it is relevant to the ascendant or descendant axis (the horizon).

Why Is This Important?

As we mentioned above, Sect is used to determine the malefic and benefic traits of the planets. The planets in the sect, or power, are more positive than those that aren't. This means that the naturally beneficial planets are even more beneficial, and those with malefic qualities are less malefic. It is believed that those planets have more "dignity," which is why they tend to behave in ways that will benefit you. As you can guess, the benefic planets that are out of power, or sect, manifest less benefic traits, and the malefic ones are even more malefic.

While this is the main way in which sect is used in astrology, the doctrine also serves as an "auspiciousness" scale for each of the planets. You can look up the diagram to better understand this concept.

Each sect contains a luminary body, either the Sun or the Moon, a benefic planet, and a malefic planet. These exclude Mercury. A sect is then used to weigh the plants' auspiciousness, determining which benefic ones will manifest even more benefic qualities and which of the malefic ones will become less malefic. Ultimately, we are left with two methods of determining the effects of the benefic and malefic planets. This depends on which sect is in power (daytime chart or nighttime chart).

The following is how the planets are ranked in each chart:

Daytime Chart

1. Jupiter
2. Venus
3. Saturn
4. Mars

Nighttime Chart

1. Venus
2. Jupiter
3. Mars
4. Saturn

Mars and Saturn are malefic planets. Saturn is less malefic in the daytime chart, and Mars is more malefic. The nighttime chart displays the opposite.

Jupiter and Venus are benefic planets. Jupiter is more benefic in the daytime chart, while Venus manifests more benefic qualities in the nighttime chart.

The Topoi

If you've ever looked at your natal chart or read about your sign's predictions for the coming year, then you probably came across the word "house." Houses are very significant in astrology, which is why you may be surprised to learn that this word ceased to exist in classical Greek astrology. The word *Topos*, which translates to place or position, was used instead. *Oikos,* which was strictly used to refer to zodiacs as signs, was Greek for *house.* This makes sense because the signs were used to describe the signs as houses for the planets. For instance, the oikos of Jupiter are Sagittarius and that of Mars in Aries. There was never a 1st oikos or a 2nd oikos like there are 1st, 2nd, 3rd, and 4th houses. The Middle Ages, however, was when all the confusion occurred. Interpreters were unsure whether the context referred to houses or signs.

That said, Whole Sign Houses are the oldest house division technique. As with most other concepts, knowledge of this form of house division was also lost during the Middle Ages. Ancient Egyptian Decanic astrology traditions, which allot a specific topic, such as children, illness, or marriage, to a certain portion of the diurnal rotation, probably influenced the creation of the 12 houses.

The Greek word *horoskopos*, which translates to hour-marker, was used to describe the ascendant. The zodiac sign that rose over the eastern horizon was "marked" by the ascendant, becoming the first whole-sign house. Any sign that entered from 0 to 30 degrees was considered the 1st house, the second one entered from 30 to 60 degrees was the second, and so on. There are 12 houses because there are 12 astrological signs. In other words, if a person's ascendant is cancer, then this sign becomes their 1st house, their 2nd house becomes Leo, and their 3rd is Virgo, etc.

The Houses

The planets that appear in our birth chart and their locations are stationary. That said, the planets are always moving, which means they inevitably change houses. Even though each planet revolves around the Sun in its own orbit, our year is 365 days long, meaning that we experience a full solar cycle that includes all the houses each year. You'll undoubtedly experience the energies of all the houses in your life.

1st House – House of Aries and Mars

This house is also known as the house of identity or self. It is representative of your physical appearance, body, behavior, social impression, health, general well-being, and temperament. The planets that occupy this house influence you significantly. For instance, a person with the Moon in the first house is known to be very emotional. Someone with Mercury in that house tends to be talkative. Planets in the 1st house determine the way others perceive you and the energy you give out. When planets make their way into this house, new projects take off, ideas flow in, goals manifest, and perspectives take shape.

2nd House – House of Taurus and Venus

This house is alternatively known as the house of money, values, or possessions. As you can tell, it corresponds to a person's finances, stability, material belongings, assets, resourcefulness, and progress. Many people don't realize that this house is also relevant to our emotions. The sense of security of a planet in the second house is determined by its material possessions. The planets that transition into this house are related to changes in a person's resources and sense of security. One can refer to this house to learn how they can become self-sufficient while adhering to their personal values.

3rd House – House of Gemini and Mercury

The 3rd house is the house of communication, education, local community, family, transportation, and short travels. It is how you share your perspectives and beliefs with others. Planets in this house encourage you to express yourself and are there for guidance on how you can enhance your relationships with those around you. When planets move into this house, new information about close friends or family may come to light.

4th House – House of Cancer and the Moon

This is the house of family, home, ancestors, and the unconscious. This planet reflects the environment in which you grew up and your experiences. This house is also associated with a person's relationship with their material figure and their general views on the idea of building a home. Planets in this house usually urge us to invest in safe spaces where we can seek protection.

5th House – House of Leo and the Sun

This is the house and creativity and pleasure. It is the hub of romance, playfulness, self-expression, and children. This house relates to your natural means of artistic expression. When planets move into the 5th house, you may experience a period of a confidence boost. This house represents anything and everything that makes you feel good.

6th House – House of Virgo and Mercury

This is the house of routine, health, wellness, and fulfillment. The house's planet determines your spending habits, life choices, and work-life balance. The house of health urges you to pay attention to your mental and physical wellness. The planets here are typically motivated by structure and organization. When planets shift into the 6th house, you may feel compelled to manage your schedule and create habits.

7th House – House of Libra and Venus

This house is that of partnership, relationships, style, and tenor. The planets in this house are concerned with all major relationships in your life, whether they're romantic, professional, or social. When planets transition into this house, you may find deals and contracts falling into place. Things may just become official!

8th House – House of Scorpio and Pluto

This is the house of regeneration, transformation, death, and sex. This house is associated with our animalistic instincts and anything that may be destructive. Birth planets in this house are usually drawn to intense relationships and occult topics. Transitionary movement into this house is associated with understanding the ins and outs of any situation. This also serves to remind us of life's challenges.

9th House – House of Sagittarius and Jupiter

This 9th house is associated with philosophy, higher education, travel, knowledge, and exploration. The planets that reside here determine how we grow our experience and integrate all our knowledge into the different aspects of life. This is a reflection of our journeys and aspirations. A movement in the 9th house involves exploring new topics, adopting different outlooks, or moving to new places.

10th House – House of Capricorn and Saturn

The 10th house is that of social status, popularity, public image, and personal authority. It determines how you initiate changes in your life and the level of determination when it comes to your goals. Career changes and revelations regarding one's ambitions typically accompany a planet's transition into the 10th house.

11th House – House of Aquarius and Uranus

This is the house of friendships and networks, and it aims to remind us of the importance of not just hard work but with whom to share the joy of our successes. Based on your aspirations and visions, the planets in this house determine the types of connections you formulate in your lifetime.

12th House – House of Pisces and Neptune

The house of the unconscious is associated with the hidden and unseen, including secrets, feelings, and even dreams. Karmic relationships are attracted into one's life when planets move into the 12th house.

Showing how numerous cultures can exist together seamlessly, the Hellenistic school of thought served as a promising foundation for the Mesopotamian astrology system. Egyptian beliefs and calendars, Babylonian techniques, and Greek philosophies were combined to create a more complex and intricate astrological system, which is very similar to the one we know today.

Chapter 7: Hellenistic Astrology II. The Zoidia

As you already know, each of the seven planets we're familiar with can be seen moving around the sky in their rightful paths. They come across numerous constellations and stars as they orbit. Make it your life's mission to observe this process, and you will see that the planets strictly wander along narrow paths in the sky - but also move along *specific constellations* - something that ancient astrologers took note of centuries ago. Thanks to them, we now know that planetary paths are ecliptic. The ecliptic can be seen as the shape of a circle that goes all around the Earth.

The Mesopotamians had already started building on this by the 5th century BCE! They divided the ecliptic circle into 12 different segments (30 degrees each). These equal segments were named the "zodiac," a word that comes from the Greek term *"zoidion."*

Even though the word "zodiac" is still relatively popular today, translating the original term "zoidion" is rather tricky because the Greek word has two very different meanings. *Zoidia*, which is the plural of *zoidion*, is derived from the word *"zoion,"* which essentially means "living being" or "animal." However, in other contexts, the word *zoion* was used to describe figures and images. It is suggested that the reason the zodiac was given this particular name can be traced back to the ancient correspondences of the signs. The duality of the word zoidia can be expressed in the fact that the zodiac signs were believed to represent images of the Ram, the Crab, the Bull, The Lion, etc.

Not only that, but this theory can be further expanded upon by exploring grammatical equivocations. The word *zion* may be a locative case suffix. In that case, a zodiac sign would be a place where something else, such as an image or a living being, is located. Another grammatical interpretation, however, may be that the word *zoidion* is a diminutive of *zoion*. This would mean that the picture or the living being would be smaller.

What Would Be a Suitable English Term?

These linguistic ambiguities make it impossible to find an equivalent English term. No similar word in the English dictionary has all these underlying themes and dual meanings. The word zoidion was used for years until a relatively suitable translation was found. At one point, the motion to use the word "signs" to refer to the zoidia was declined. When we trace the English word "signs" back to its Latin origins (signum), we'll find that it was originally meant to refer to images or pictures. However, today, the word is used to denote a broader range of connotations that its initial meaning is no longer as accurate as it used to be. Later, it was decided that using the word "image" to refer to the zodion was the most reasonable option. The concept behind it is that you can use this translation as a base when referring to the "image of the Lion," "image of the Ram," "image of the Bull," etc.

The idea of using the word "image" is practical because you can refer to the zoidia in an abstract sense. In most cases, when dealing with astronomy and astrology, there are many concepts, especially ones that we can understand, that we can perceive with our minds even when we don't necessarily see them with our eyes. The way we comprehend particular *zoidia* is guided by real visual images of the constellations. However, ancient astrologers like Ptolemy did not rely on real-time images of the sky and constellations. This is particularly the case with astrologers who use the tropical or moving zodiac. Instead, they relied on the abstract division and segments of the ecliptic, which we mentioned above. These divisions were believed to be correspondents with specific qualities.

If you delve deep into ancient astrology, you'll find that many texts use the word "twelfth-parts," or *dodekatemoria*, to refer to the zodiac signs. This way, astrologers represented each sign as an abstract segment of the ecliptic. Since each segment or division was believed to be associated with specific qualities, astrologers thought that the divisions were able to give signals, omens, or even prophecies for certain events. This may explain why our modern understanding of the word "sign" no longer denotes an image or a picture but extends to refer to symbols, signals, and indications.

You probably think that we've gone off on a tangent here. What do these linguistic obscurities have to do with astrology and *zoidia*? Well, the evolution of the word "sign" is very similar to how this entire concept is applied in ancient Greco-Roman astrology. These mysteries, and paradoxes, even, have paved the way for an entirely novel understanding of the concept in modern-day astrological practices.

In the 1st century BCE, Varro, a Roman polymath, explained that signs and constellations refer to the same things. Constellations and signs are synonymous because constellations signify something. For instance, Libra is associated with or rather signifies the equinox. For simplicity, the term "signs" (of the zodiac) can be appropriately used for *zoidia*.

Now that you know where the term "zodiac signs" came from and what the zoidia essentially is, we'll delve deep into the origin of the zodiac signs. Here, you'll learn how ancient Greek astrologers used them and how they're different from the ones we use today.

Qualities of the Zoidia

The foundation of the zodiac is primarily built on Mesopotamian tradition. That said, the qualities that later astrologers started assigning to each sign originated in the Hellenistic tradition. According to Hellenistic astrology, one of the most significant roles that the zodiac signs take on is that they influence the way that the implications of the planet appear in the chart. The signs of the zodiac can do so through the following main qualities:

- Having rulership over the planet
- Their gender (this is something that we no longer rely on in modern astrology)

- Triplicity (this has evolved into elements in modern-day astrology)
- Quadruplicity

Numerous other diversified qualities rely on how the constellations look. However, in most cases, these are ancillary qualities to account for and are often used within the framework of certain techniques.

Unlike modern astrology, the concept of systematic borrowing wasn't popular in Hellenistic astrology. This means that the implications of the zodiac signs and those of the twelve houses we discussed in the previous chapters weren't interchangeable; ancient astrologers didn't believe Aries to be synonymous with the 1st house or Leo to be equivalent to the 5th house. The idea of borrowing from a house's implications to obtain those of a certain sign wasn't there.

The Names of the Signs

As you already know, each of the twelve signs has a unique name. The name of each sign comes from its constellation. The zodiac is decorated with 12 bright images of the Ram, followed by the Bull, and then the Twins. The Crab, the Lion, and the Maiden come next. The Claws, which was later renamed the Scales, lies next to the Maiden, and beside it comes the Scorpion. The Archer, the Goat-Horned One, the Water-Bearer, and the Fishes are the last in the zodiac.

While it would make more sense to give the name "The Claws" to a sign like Cancer or Scorpio, for instance, you may be surprised to learn that this was the ancient name of Libra. This is because it was believed to represent a portion of the claws of the constellation next to it (the Scorpion). However, when ancient astrologers started differentiating between both zodiac signs, they renamed Libra "the Scales." If you happen to stumble across an ancient Hellenistic astrology text, you'll find that the term "the Claws" refers to Libra. It was also used in a poetic context.

The following are the Greek names for each of the zodiac signs, along with their meanings:

1. **Aries:** Krios (The Ram)
2. **Taurus:** Tauros (The Bull)
3. **Gemini:** Didumoi (The Twins)
4. **Cancer:** Karkinos (The Crab)
5. **Leo:** Leon (The Lion)
6. **Virgo:** Parthenos (The Maiden)
7. **Libra:** Zugos (The Scales)
8. **Scorpio:** Skorpios (The Scorpion)
9. **Sagittarius:** Toxotes (The Archer)
10. **Capricorn:** Aigokeros (The Goat-Horned One)
11. **Aquarius:** Hudrochoos (The Water-Pourer)
12. **Pisces:** Ichthues (The Fishes)

As you can tell, the English terms for the signs don't look remotely similar to the Greek words (except for Taurus, Leo, and Scorpio) because, to a great extent, the English terms come from the Latin translations of the original Greek words. For instance, the word ram is Aries in Latin, "bull" is Taurus, etc. You will commonly find Greek writings translated literally. This means that upon reading translated astrological text, you may find the zodiac signs referred to as "the Maiden," "the Scales," "the Bull," and so on.

How Ancient Greek Astrologers Used the Zodiac

Ancient Greek astrologers applied their understanding of the zodiac signs to numerous aspects of our being and life in general. While many of these concepts are still applied today or serve as a foundation for modern-day studies, others have been rejected.

Gender Identification

Ancient Greek astrologers believed that the zodiac signs could be split into two groups based on gender: masculine and feminine. Starting at the first sign, which is Aries, the odd ones were believed to be masculine, and the even ones, which begin at Taurus, were thought to be feminine.

Every well-known Hellenistic astrologer accepted this practice. This doctrine was popular to the point where Sextus Empiricus assumed that the Pythagorean practice of naming the odd numbers "male" and the even numbers "female" was influenced by the astrologers of the time. While the association is correct, the Pythagorean theory of the numerology of gender is likely older than the gender assignment of the zodiac signs.

Either way, this Hellenistic astrological tradition was often used to identify or predict genders. According to Sextus, it was believed that the masculine and feminine signs could influence the birth of either males or females. Valens also mentioned that the zodiac sign's gender, which includes planetary indicators for siblings, can help determine the gender of the person's siblings. For instance, if Jupiter, the Sun, and Mercury reside in a masculine sign, brothers are granted. He also suggested that the gender of the signs can be used to determine which of the person's parents will die first. Firmicus also wrote about the birth of twins, where the gender of the signs can be used to determine the sex of the babies.

The assignment of gender to the zodiac signs wasn't only used for gender identification purposes. It was also used as a descriptive aspect in numerous sources. For example, feminine signs were believed to be passive, and masculine signs were perceived as more active. While the former was conceptualized as subordinate, adjectives like "commanding" and "authoritative" were associated with the latter. As you can tell, these correspondences mainly denote gender norms and roles. This doctrine also determined where a person lies in the gender spectrum and whether the native tends to transgress traditional expectations and gender norms.

In modern-day astrology, we no longer use the zodiac signs to predict the gender of the native or where they stand on the gender spectrum. This is perhaps why the concept of masculine and feminine zodiac signs has declined in popularity.

Body Part Assignment

Zodiacal Melothesia, the practice of assigning body parts to each sign, was another common practice among ancient Greek Astrologers. This arrangement is still popular today. The underlying belief behind this practice is that there is a system of sympathetic connections between the human body's microcosm, which reflects the macrocosm of the alignment of the universe during the time of birth.

All systems of body part assignments begin at the top of the human body, where Aries is assigned to the head. The system then continues labeling the other body parts in order of the signs, all the way down to the feet assigned to Pisces (the last zodiac sign). Numerous illustrations of this doctrine were drawn up, which is why it became known as Homo Signorum, or Man of Signs. The assignment structure is more or less the same. However, you may find some discrepancies in the torso area.

The following is the standard assignment of body parts to the signs:

1. **Aries** - The head
2. **Taurus** - The neck
3. **Gemini** - The shoulders, arms, and hands
4. **Cancer** - The chest
5. **Leo** - The ribs, sides, and heart
6. **Virgo** - The belly and abdomen
7. **Libra** - The hips and buttocks
8. **Scorpio** - The genitalia
9. **Sagittarius** - The thighs
10. **Capricorn** - The knees
11. **Aquarius** - The lower legs
12. **Pisces** - The feet

Ancient astrologers used this system to determine the body parts that might be susceptible to injuries and illnesses. Dorotheus suggests that a mathematical technique used to determine a Lot of Injuries, which is a point derived from Saturn and Mars, can be used to predict injury. The native would experience an ailment in the body part corresponding to the sign on which this point falls in the natal chart. This doctrine was further applied in astrological medicine, where practitioners used this concept to determine potential treatments.

General Predictions

This practice is no longer used in modern astrology because it lacks logic and rationale. Ancient astrologers used the zodiac signs to make general predictions, which were often based on irregular patterns or considerations. Ancient interpreters sometimes used certain techniques and general contexts to make predictions. For instance, some signs were considered fertile, while others were considered barren. Astrologers used this concept to determine whether a native would experience difficulties with reproduction. It's important to note that these qualities and characteristics were not standardized, meaning that not all Hellenistic astrologers used the same guidelines and techniques to make their predictions. This is why the qualities were often reported with slight discrepancies.

This level of variability makes it impossible to fully or accurately disclose what the different signs meant in terms of fate or the future. However, the following is a general overview of the qualities and characteristics commonly associated with each sign:

- **Enigmatical**: Sagittarius and Capricorn.
- **Incomplete**: Taurus, Virgo, Sagittarius, and Capricorn
- **Four-footed**: Aries, Taurus, Leo, and Sagittarius.
- **Human in Form**: Gemini, Virgo, Libra, Sagittarius, and Aquarius.
- **Prolific** (abundance in terms of off-spring): Cancer, Scorpio, and Pisces.
- **Barren** (sterile): Gemini, Virgo, Sagittarius, and Capricorn.
- **Royal or king-like**: Aries, Leo, and Sagittarius.

Qualities like mute, vocal, and outrageous were also used to determine the nature of the signs. The constellations and their associated images influenced these characteristics and other rationales or beliefs.

The Ancient Greek *Zoidia* and the associated doctrines and beliefs have largely contributed to our understanding of astrology. Not only did they shape modern-day practices, but they also provided a sturdy basis for additional research. While today's practitioners reject some ancient concepts, others are still widely practiced and accepted.

Chapter 8: The Thema Mundi and Hellenistic Charts

In this chapter, we will go over the concept of "Thema Mundi," analyze its origins and explain why it is vital in Hellenistic astrology. The second part highlights the differences between Hellenistic charts and modern astrological ones. We will also explain how you can transform a modern birth chart into a Hellenistic one.

What Is "Thema Mundi?"

Astrology involves the study of celestial objects and their movements. It is mainly used to predict things that will happen in different people's lives based on the position of the Moon, Sun, planets, and stars. Astrology started due to human beings' attempts to record, measure, and predict seasonal fluctuations mainly caused by positional changes of cosmic objects.

The "Thema Mundi" is known as the birth chart of the world since it was an ancient method used to understand the fundamental principles in astrology. The chart below illustrates the Thema Mundi, which marked the origin of the traditional zodiac sign system.

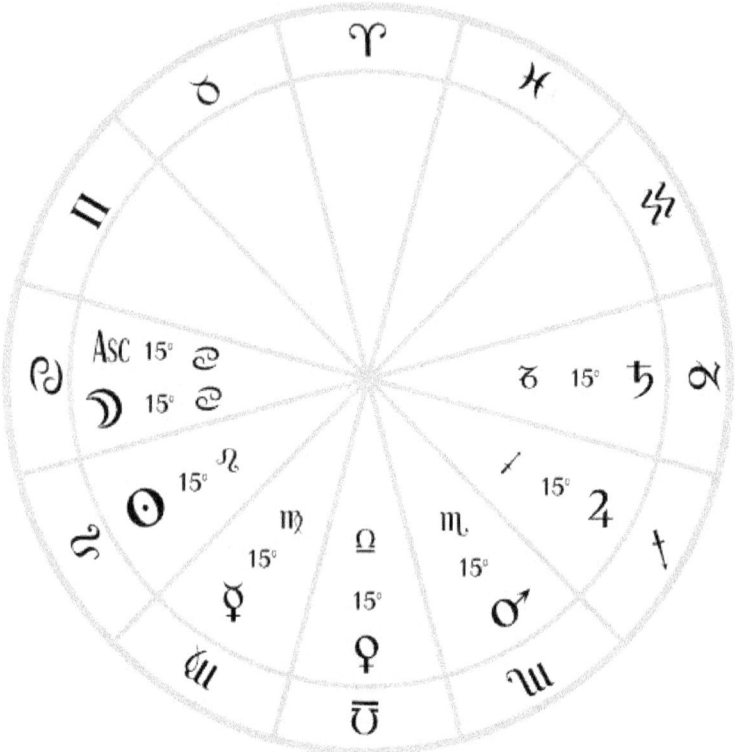

Thema Mundi.
I, Meredith Garstin, CC BY-SA 3.0 <http://creativecommons.org/licenses/by-sa/3.0/>, via Wikimedia Commons https://upload.wikimedia.org/wikipedia/commons/7/74/Thema_Mundi.svg

The signs of the horoscope marked the birth of the world that later came to be known as the Thema Mundi. It was used as a conceptual device or teaching tool in Hellenistic astrology. The system offered a rationale for the sign rulership and specific significations of the signs commonly used.

There were some variations surrounding the Thema Mundi, but all versions have Cancer as the Ascendant. The rest of the other visible planets fan out following a zodiacal order based on factors like speed and distance from the Sun.

According to the traditional rulerships based on the Thema Mundi, the Moon Rules Cancer, whereas Leo is ruled by the Sun. The Thema Mundi refers to "theme," and it also means chart. It was used as a horoscope in Hellenistic astrology that showed the positions of the only visible celestial bodies, including the Moon and Sun, before the invention of the telescope. The Thema Mundi reflects the logic behind aspects like exaltations, sign rulerships, and different meanings of other things.

There was some form of confusion during the late Middle Ages when the horoscope was confused with the Thema Mundi. The Hellenistic chart moves away from believing signs and houses are directly correlated. Modern astrology believes that the first sign of Aries is correlated to the first house. However, Cancer is the ascendant in the Thema Mundi, which significantly differs from modern astrology.

Why Is Thema Mundi Important in Hellenistic Astrology?

The Thema Mundi is believed to show the ideal position of the luminaries and the planets. If you are unfamiliar with the theme and want to learn astrology, you can use the world chart. Since time immemorial, it has been used as a teaching device for astrologers. The symbolic chart of planets shows their positions at the beginning of humankind's existence.

The chart was first used in teaching astrology in the Hellenistic times, as well as traditional sources from Arabic, Greek, and Persian origins used to represent the Birth-chart. It was used as a model for the evolving theories that developed over the centuries.

Another reason why the Thema Mundi is important is that it provides details about the meanings of the seven original planets that appear on the chart. It also discusses the role of these planets in the astrology chart and in general times of life. The Thema Mundi highlights different life processes, including the four qualities and the roots, and finishes the journey with the twelve zodiac signs and houses. The chart also helps practitioners in the field of astrology gain a deeper understanding of its origins.

The Thema Mundi chart provides the positions of the two luminaries, including the Moon and Sun, and the positions of the other planets. It demonstrates the logic behind planetary exaltations and the rulership signs to give you insight into the placement of different bodies during the time of creation. The chart does not correlate with any astronomical event since Mercury and Venus are located very far from the Sun.

It is believed that Thema Mundi came into existence around 322B.C, and it has played a key role in Hellenistic astrology. The theme is still relevant today since it is ideal for novices in astrology looking for ways to evaluate different circumstances. You can also use it to plan for future events, especially if you need guidance. Most astrologers who operated during the early modern civilizations were primarily concerned with fate than individual ambitions. Therefore, not every component of the chart in traditional astrology matters to you. However, reading Hellenistic astrology can go a long way in helping you work out your circumstances, resolve past events, and prepare for the things likely to come in the future.

You can significantly benefit from Hellenistic astrology since it comprises three major subdivisions. The first one is universal astrology, and it is used to predict specific events that are likely to affect many people, like natural disasters or weather-related incidents like tsunamis or floods. It can also be used to predict man-made crises like wars or genocide.

Natal astrology is the second subdivision, and it involves using an individual date and time of birth to create a birth chart. It determines your personality and the paths you are likely to take in life. Katarchic astrology helps individuals pick the best time to perform different activities according to their charts. It can also help you pick the appropriate date for special occasions like weddings.

Different aspects of Hellenistic astrology are relevant today and used in various branches of astrology. However, Hellenistic astrology is set aside from other types by the concept of houses which is still practiced today. Birth charts are used today to determine someone's horoscope and path. Hellenistic astrology also led to the development of the concept of Lots consisting of more than 12. A Lot of Fortune is probably the most important.

What Is the Main Difference between Hellenistic Charts and Modern Astrological Ones?

The main roots of Hellenistic astrology date back to the 18th Century BC Babylon. The Babylon records of the celestial objects are the oldest documents followed in the Western world regarding astrological studies. During the 4th Century, a Hellenistic Greek astrological system was born, which can be traced to the Greek mathematician Ptolemy in the 2nd century AD. The Hellenistic chart was developed, and it includes seven planets, whereas the modern astrological charts have 12 planets, 12 signs of the zodiac, and 12 houses.

Hellenistic charts are a system used to predict events likely to occur in the life of someone, a group of people, or a state. The predictions are obtained through calculations based on movements as well as positions of celestial bodies in the face of cosmic objects that are permanently fixed. The main planets are Mars, Venus, Jupiter, Saturn, Mercury, the sun, and the moon. Planets like Neptune, Pluto, and Uranus were only added to the natal chart following the advent of the telescope. These three planets were excluded from the Hellenistic chart since they were believed to be too far away and could not influence worldly events.

Hellenistic astrology focuses on the outer world and precise predictions of various concrete events, whereas modern astrology focuses on the inner world. Modern astrology is based on natal astrology, which involves using a client's birth chart to help provide psychological counseling. The tropical zodiac is used in modern astrology to focus on future events that may happen in the life of individuals. According to this concept, the Sun greatly influences the events that occur on Earth since it is at the center of the solar system. The relationship between the Sun and the Earth forms the basis of modern astrology.

In modern astrology, all the calculations are determined by the subject's date of birth. This kind of astrology is horoscopic, and the sky is divided to create 88 constellations along the sun's path, which are used for calculations. In a modern chart, 12 signs are used to calculate the position of the Sun when the individual involved was born. It also involved 12 planets and 12 houses that are believed to correlate.

Modern chart points represent different layers of the self, which can be explained using different interpretations like the houses and the planets. On the other hand, Hellenistic chart points show circumstances and people beyond your control. The chart focuses on the bigger picture.

Another notable aspect of modern charts is that they are readily available on the internet and in books. They are easy to understand compared to the complex Hellenistic charts. To understand a Hellenistic chart, you may need to consult an experienced astrologer.

How to Transform a Modern Birth Chart into a Hellenistic One?

Astrology has been used for thousands of years to record or tell time. The Bible and the Quran refer to specific lunar phases to mark specific dates and months in the year. Many civilizations also used the lunar calendar. A birth chart believed to be the oldest with more than 2000 years was discovered in a cave. This shows that people developed an interest in using astrology as an effective tool to unlock knowledge about individuals long ago.

In modern times, birth charts continue to be used to give us a deeper understanding of ourselves and how we relate with others in the world around us. If you are interested in transforming your modern birth chart into a Hellenistic one, it is a good idea to generate your chart using the whole sign system.

First and foremost, you must know your date of birth, year, time, and place before you cast your chart. You can easily interpret your birth chart when you have all the information. However, you must choose a reliable online application to help you get the chart you want. You can get it for free if you carefully look through astrology sites.

When you visit a site like Astrodienst that offers free services to create your chart, click on the create horoscope as a guest user. You need to enter your details, including name, gender, date of birth, time of birth, town, and country where you were born. If you have the time of birth, the entire process becomes much easier.

Under the Ascendant Horoscope chart drawings, click chart drawing and continue. You'll see your accurate and correct sign and all other astrological details below your name. If you want a free one, this is one of the easiest ways of getting it. You will see that the birth chart comes in the form of a wheel, and it should move counter-clockwise starting from the letter ascendant or AC. For instance, if Virgo rules your ascendant or 1st house, the natural planetary ruler is Mercury. This reflects a patient and analytical personality. Mars is the action planet, and it also comes in the first house in Libra. The energy helps create an active vibe.

The second house means your financial issues are in safe hands, and Libra rules the house. Partnerships will improve your finances. As you go through every house, you'll get the interpretation and meaning of every single one.

The Benefits of Mapping Your Astrological Birth Chart

There are many benefits to mapping your astrological birth chart since it helps you know the exact moment you were born. The zodiac is commonly used since it has 12 signs and 12 houses. Each zodiac sign has a different meaning, and each house shows a different aspect of our lives, including family, education, health, love, and work.

The zodiac chart also has the Sun and Moon on top of the ten planets used by astrologers to understand an individual's psyche. If you map out the planet and zodiac signs in a specific astrological house during the time you were born, you can better understand who you are.

The "Thema Mundi" is known as the theme or birth chart of the world since it is one of the oldest methods used to understand different principles in astrology. The Thema Mundi and Hellenistic charts have evolved and are still relevant today. Although the astrological birth or natal chart comprising 12 houses, 12 signs, and 12 planets is commonly used to predict individual life, Hellenistic astrology is still relevant.

Chapter 9: The Hermetic Lots

In this chapter, we will focus on the concept of astrological lots. We will explain how they are believed to be pre-Hellenistic and explore their Hermetic nature. The chapter also explains who Hermes Trismegistus was to astrology. The second part outlines the names and provides instructions for calculating the seven lots. The formulas are based on diurnal and nocturnal charts.

The Hermetic Lots

The Hermetic lots include a set of seven lots. Each lot is linked to one of the seven visible planets, or to the Moon, or the Sun. These lots were attributed to Hermes Trismegistus, who contributed critically to the Hellenistic astrology traditions. The lots can be used to assign topics to houses where the symbolism of the Ascendant and planetary configurations is all crucial to lots. They form a critical component of chart delineation. In the absence of lots, we fail to get the necessary confirmation to gain confidence in what the natal chart indicates.

Background

Lots were mainly used in Hellenistic and medieval astrology, but it is somehow not prioritized in modern astrology. Even today, it seems that astrologers do not use lots regularly. They are mainly misunderstood today due to the marginalization they suffered in

European Renaissance astrology. The lots were very popular in ancient astrology.

During the time of William Lilly in the 17th century, the astrologers continued to only use a Lot of Fortune. However, ancient astrologers believe this fortune was used strangely. Lilly's method was known as "Fortuna," which has continued in modern astrology, although it is misunderstood and rarely used. The Lot Fortune remains important since it is used in today's horary practice.

Who Was Hermes Trismegistus in the Tradition of Astrology?

Hermes Trismegistus (thrice-great Hermes) came from the combination of the wisdom gods Thoth and Hermes, and it is regarded as one of the most difficult to understand figures of intellectual history. In Hellenistic Egypt, Thoth was given the name *Hermes*. The "wise Egyptian" has also been associated with magical and mystical writings such as astrology, alchemy, the transcendence of God, and medicine.

Hermes Trismegistus.
See page for author, CC BY 4.0 <https://creativecommons.org/licenses/by/4.0>, via Wikimedia Commons
https://commons.wikimedia.org/wiki/File:Hermes_Trismegistus_illustration_Wellcome_L 0016507.jpg

According to the Euhemeristic fashion, Hermes may also be explained as the son of the god. Historians leave the speculation to occultism and alchemy. Hermes Trismegistus is celebrated as the founder of philosophy by the philosophers of the Renaissance, while Freemasons viewed him as their forefather. Hermes is regarded as one of the biggest occult figures and is also associated with the esoteric. His teachings are believed to have influenced the Christian and Muslim versions of religion.

Predicting with Lots

Lots can be used in predictive work, solar returns, planetary years, transits, and places. They also significantly multiplied during the Medieval period due to the growing interest in mundane astrology. Many related to specific weather patterns, political activities, and commodities are used with mundane predictions.

Several lots are mentioned in Hellenistic texts, and their meanings can be confusing since there may be alternative lots with the same meaning. In the Hellenistic period, there were about 12 very popular lots, most of which related to family matters and general issues about life. In Medieval astrology, the lots continued to be used. We will focus on the seven most important lots in this chapter and provide formulas for calculating them.

The lot formula follows a sequence from A to B, meaning the lots move between these points during the day and cover the reverse distance at night. The distance "from A to B" is projected from the Ascendant, meaning this is the diurnal formula used to calculate the lot. The following are the calculations of the common lots.

The Lot of Fortune

Fortune is the most famous lot, and it is also known as the Lot of the Moon. It is renowned for things of a physical nature or circumstances surrounding the body. We calculate Fortune by taking the distance from the sect light where the Sun is above the horizon to the non-sect light referring to the Moon when the Sun is below the horizon. Follow the distance from the Ascendant and observe the degree and the house it lands in.

The formula for Lot of Fortune is:

- **Day Chart:** Ascendant + Moon Sun
- **Night Chart:** Ascendant - Moon + Sun

The sun can be above the horizon, affecting the chart massively. You must reverse the measurement between the moon and the sun at night. When plotting, you'll obtain the arch by measuring from the moon to the sun, using the signs for direction.

Fortune is not only about money and luck. We can better think of it as chance and situation. Fortune is commonly used to signify the things that can befall you outside your control, especially if they relate to health. The Lot of Fortune was used in other quarters to represent fortune, body, and health. Astrologers used a fortune to indicate wealth or material well-being, whereas the horary charts use it to mark success.

However, Fortune alone is not a perfect indicator of health and wealth. It has its place when it comes to delineating each topic. Fortune can be used as a predictive factor concerning occurrences involving finances or the body.

Success or wealth is a complex matter to determine and is based on other factors like fixed stars. Fortune can indicate something that will turn out to be the opposite of the current situation.

The Lot of Spirit

The Lot of Fortune is concerned with the body, well-being, fortune, and health of the person involved. The formula for the Lot of Spirit is the reverse of the one used for the Lot of Fortune. The formulas are as follows:

- **Day Chart:** Ascendant - Moon + Sun
- **Night Chart:** Ascendant + Moon - Sun

The calculation of the Lot of Spirit is opposite to Fortune and distant from the ascendant, which means they complement each other. Connected to creativity and your will—can show how you will act and control yourself when dealing with certain situations.

Just like Fortune, the Spirit has a meaning closely related to the Ascendant, especially the significations of character and capability. The significations are more commonly associated with the house ruler than the place. The spirit figures involved in Hellenistic treatments include temperament, character, and professional aptitude. It also ventures into the analysis of mental and bodily ailments in Valens. Social and mental circumstances are the common denominators to all the significations, although health is not completely overlooked.

The Lot of Necessity

The Lot of Necessity signifies submissions, constraints, struggles, hatreds, enmities, wars, and all other restrictive things that can befall people as a result of their birth. It is also known as the Lot of Poverty, the Lot of Mercury, or the Lot of Small-mindedness.

The following formula represents the Lot:

- **Day Chart:** Ascendant + Fortune − Mercury
- **Night Chart:** Ascendant + Mercury − Fortune

The Lot of Necessity is not very common in Hellenistic astrology, but it is one of the most effective, according to Valens. The opposite of this particular lot is the Lot of Love. The significations of the Lot Necessity are connected to negative associations and are also linked to Mercury. It relates to how one addresses the issue of challengers, competitors, adversaries, and enemies.

When the law is in a good state, it reflects things like the prevailing competition, disputes, and fair treatment of the law. The lot shows attacks from adversaries, legal challenges, unfair treatment, and hatred in its bad state. Love focuses on different types of relationships we pursue, and Necessity relates to the relationships we need to deal with or rather avoid.

The Lot of Eros

The Lot of Eros, Lot of Love, Lot of Desire, or Lot of Venus. It signifies the appetites we have for mutual favor and friendship. Its formula is:

- **Day Chart:** Ascendant + Venus − Spirit
- **Night Chart:** Ascendant + Spirit − Venus

The opposite of the Lot of Love is the Lot of Necessity. These two lots have a special relationship. The significations of Love are connected to those of Venus and the 7th Place. The lot mainly pertains to friendship, desire, and enjoyable associations and alliances. Sympathy between the signs of equal ascension is usually more robust if it is in the charts with sympathetic crosses. Love was used for delineating sexuality, friendship, and what people usually do for pleasure.

The Lot of Courage

The formula for Lot of Courage is represented as follows:

- **Day Chart:** Ascendant + Fortune − Mars
- **Night Chart:** Ascendant + Mars − Fortune

In this lot, courage significantly contributes to boldness, might, treachery, and villainy. This sign is based on Mars and provides traits of fortitude to the natives. It is based on the physical body or fortune as well as the actions of Mars. When this lot is placed in the house, it seems to reflect our worst fears and the things we should face. However, with enough courage, you can overcome some of these challenges regardless of fear. Dealing with different situations in life can be challenging, which is why you must have the nerve to face any situation you may encounter.

The Lot of Victory

The Lot of Victory is based on Jupiter and significantly contributes to trust, good expectations, associations, and contests. Its formula is the following:

- **Day Lot:** Ascendant + Jupiter − Spirit
- **Night Lot:** Ascendant + Spirit − Jupiter

While victory is associated with good things such as rewards, it can sometimes contribute to penalties. The penalty is punishment, and it is something that should not be cherished. Therefore, it is a good idea to use this lot to predict positive things that can turn your life around. When approaching different things, you must have a positive attitude and good expectations in whatever you do.

When you achieve your goals, you must show appreciation and gratitude to enjoy them for a long period. Some people fail to attain their goals because of the general fear of the unknown. If you don't have a formidable plan, you may experience different problems in your journey to obtain the things you want. However, nothing is impossible, and you can use this lot to get inspiration.

The Lot of Nemesis

The Lot of Nemesis is based on Saturn, reflecting the different things most likely to impact the natives. If you want to achieve a certain goal, there are a lot of things that can bring you down. For instance, negative publicity or unfavorable media coverage can be your downfall. The formula for this lot is:

- **Day Chart:** Ascendant + Fortune − Saturn
- **Night Lot:** Ascendant + Saturn − Fortune

This lot can contribute to subterranean fates and ice-cold results like impotence, grief, destruction, exile, and quality of death. The following are some of the inescapable aspects that can affect you. In Aries, elements like impatience or the sword in Taurus.

It is vital to understand your sign and the things that are likely to affect you in your endeavor to achieve different goals. In Gemini, the media, slander, and duplicitous lifestyle are some of the issues you must be wary of. Insecurity, getting lost, and large crowds are the major things you should look out for. Pride and arrogance are some major issues you should be aware of if you belong to Leo.

When it comes to Virgo, jumping to conclusions and lacking faith may be your greatest enemies. In Libra, you should be aware of aspects like separation and divorce. In Scorpio, jealousy, murder, plots, and lack of trust are the major threats you can experience. In Capricorn, neglect and carelessness should not characterize your life if you want positive results.

Lots were used in Hellenistic and Medieval astrology, and each lot is linked to the visible planets. These lots were attributed to Hermes, who significantly contributed to Hellenistic astrology. The main function of lots is to help astrologers assign different topics to houses on the birth chart to help the individuals involved predict different things that can impact their lives. Lots form a crucial aspect of chart delineation. Without lots, we may encounter challenges related to interpreting houses and other components in the birth charts.

Chapter 10: Ancient Hellenistic Techniques

In the previous chapter, we covered the Lots. This one will look at the other six important Hellenistic techniques. These include the rising decan, the lord of nativity, dispositors of nativity, planets/lords in the houses, the application and separation of the moon, and the 12th harmonic. We provide a detailed explanation for each concept to help the readers understand its application.

The Rising Decan

Have you ever thought about why people who belong to the same zodiac sign are different? All individuals with the Sun in Aries are different, and the entire birth chart determines this. Ancient astrologers divided each zodiac sign into divisions known as decans or decanates. The zodiac signs are divided using the method of triplicities, including any three of the four classical elements, namely water, air, fire, and earth. Each zodiac sign is, therefore, subdivided into three equal parts consisting of ten degrees each.

If you want to understand different things taking place in your life, it might be necessary to know these decans. The decans have proven effective, especially in predictive astrology in the horoscope. The ruler of the rising decan in a particular sign on the chart dramatically influences the entire life if the ruler makes any meaningful elements during the time in question. The influence of the decan affects different aspects of the zodiac.

A natal chart has twelve zodiac signs, meaning each sign occupies 30 degrees. The twelve signs constitute 360 degrees to create a complete natal chart. Each sign is subdivided into three decans consisting of 10 degrees. Each decan consists of a ruler that becomes a sub-ruler of that particular sign. When you familiarize yourself with the triplicities, including earth, fire, water, and air, it becomes easier to know the sub-rulers for each particular decan. Each sign's decan belongs to the same triplicity, coming in the same order as in the zodiac. For instance, Aries is the first decan of Aries, and it is ruled by Mars, whereas the second decan is Leo, which is ruled by the Sun. Therefore, the second decan of Aries is also ruled by the Sun. You should know that each decan belonging to the same triplicity, in this case, has a fire element.

The Aries decans as follows:

First Decan Aries: From March 21 to 30th, 0 degrees to 10 degrees and is ruled by Mars. The first decan is the most energetic and influenced by Mars. The people who belong to this decan can excite other people around them and have an endearing childlike innocence. They have great enthusiasm and want to live to the fullest.

Second Decan Aries: From March 31st to April 9th, 10 degrees to 20 degrees and is ruled by the Sun. The second decan consists of rays from the Sun, and the individuals who belong to this decan will maintain their aims, principles, and ambitions even under trying conditions. They are focused, and this helps them focus on the bigger picture.

Third Decan Aries: From April 10th to 20th, 20 degrees to 30 degrees and is ruled by Jupiter. This third decan consists of rays from Jupiter. It is bold, eager, and shows signs of always wanting to be first. The individuals who belong to this decan are intellectuals with a strong sense of individualism. They try hard to avoid scenarios where they are forced to conform to or adopt the herd mentality. They are independent and smart enough not to fall for other people's demands.

The Lord of Nativity

One planet, the Ruler of the Horoscope, or Chart Ruler, is described as the Lord of the Nativity, and this is the Lord of the Ascendant. However, specific rules are used to determine the Lord of the first house. A poorly aspected Lord of the Ascendant in an uncongenial sign can be replaced by a planet that is more elevated if it exists. Other planets should be considered to determine the Lord of the Nativity using the two approaches outlined below:

First Approach
1. If the planet is angular, the Lord becomes the domicile lord of the Midheaven.
2. The planet found in the Midheaven (or 10th House) is the Lord. If there is no planet in the Midheaven, the Lord becomes a planet found in the 11th house.

Second Approach
Other planets can also become Lord of the Nativity when the following conditions exist.
1. The planet is the domicile lord of the Ascendant.
2. The planet within the rising sign with links to the Ascendant.
3. The Lord of the Moon.
4. The Lot of Fortune.
5. If a planet can be in heliacal (the last phase of a planet) - setting, rising, or retrograde within a space of seven days of birth. In the event of multiple planets, the one not under the beams will be the preferred choice.
6. The prenatal lunation can be the bound lord.

The Lord of the Nativity is generally viewed as the plane with the following features.

- Can rise out from the beams of the Sun
- According to the zodiacal rulership, a planet that has more dignity or is more familiar with its location.
- It must be the most powerful depending on its configuration concerning other stars in the chart.
- It should be the most powerful in relation to the nativity figure.

Dispositors of Nativity

The Natal ruler or the Lord of that particular house is the dispositor. The term dispositor means "arranger" in Latin or also refers to the process of setting order. In astrology, a dispositor is known as a planet capable of disposing of another planet. In other words, that planet wields more power or influences the planet because it is found in its house. Dispose also means to arrange or regulate.

When the Lord is placed by a sign found within a particular chart, this shows the sign's influence on the cusp. The placement of the lord by the house within the same chart also shows related areas that control the house's affairs. The Lord of the First house is known as the Lord of the Ascendant. The aspects that exist between the dispositors of the two houses show how the connections in their affairs influence the individual's life.

If the Lord of one house is posited in another, mutual house reception happens. This pairing combines the affairs and shows the links between the two houses involved. The situation is similar to planetary mutual reception, where the energies in the affairs of the two houses are shared.

Planets/Lords in the Houses

The birth chart is more like a snapshot reflecting the connection between the Earth, other planets, and your life. The chart consists of 12 houses, representing where the real action of your life takes place. The date, time, and location of your birth will point to the sign that will rule the house on your chart. The rulership can be attributed to the zodiac signs or the points of a house where they intersect on the wheel.

The house is the grounding force of astrology when it comes to Earthly matters. For instance, each house is associated with different aspects of life like career, love, relationships, and home. Knowing your house will help you gain a deeper understanding of yourself. The houses can also give your insight into different things that might happen to you. If you can predict certain things in your life, you can take corrective measures to prepare for anything.

The zodiac wheel starts with the first house or Ascendant, which represents the position of the Sun where it rose during the time of your birth. The sun governs yourself, your first impression, and your identity. The houses move anti-clockwise around the zodiacal wheel. They encompass broad themes of family, society, and other elements that affect our lives in many ways.

When different planets move around the Sun and the zodiac sign, they pass through the houses. For example, when the planet Venus passes through Aries during the time of your birth, and it is in your first house of individuality, then topics like confidence and self-love will feature prominently in your lifetime. As a result, astrologers make different chart interpretations based on signs, planets, and the houses in your birth chart.

When it comes to the first six houses are known as "personal houses" since they govern various aspects of daily life, family, and community. The last six houses are known as "interpersonal houses" since they control experiences that include relationships, career, travel, and friendships. These components influence our lives in many ways, and they often determine the outcomes of different things we do in life.

For instance, the first house concerns beginnings and dictates the origins of identity and the self, your new endeavors, and outward appearance. The zodiac sign that regulates your chart's first house is the ascendant or the rising sign. Therefore, the first house is significant since it determines how you present yourself to others and how they perceive you. The self in each individual creates first impressions of other people, which are vital since they spell out how you will relate to them. Other houses also define other characteristics that shape you. You must know your house in your natal chart to better understand yourself.

The Application

Ancient Hellenistic techniques were designed in a way that they would help people study different aspects of their lives using celestial objects. If you want to look for insights into your natal chart or daily horoscope, you can use any of the many available astrology apps. For instance, different types of astrology books and other online applications provide a wide range of information about the

Earth, stars, and other planets.

There are free options you can get, and these provide details about zodiac-related information that help you better understand yourself. The Moon calendar is another simple version that allows you to track the cycles of the Moon and incorporate its phases into your daily routine. The Moon phases mean different things you can apply in your life. You can also learn different astrological lessons by observing the changes in the world around you.

The 12th Harmonic

The 12th harmonic charts are part of modern astrology since they employ advanced astrological methods. Harmonic astrology consists of a detailed interpretation of different energies broken down from natal aspects to a chart. The 12th harmonic is regarded as the secondary self. The connection of the Duads to the natal shows that the 12th Harmonic is very accurate.

The 12th Harmonic reveals different aspects about people, such as channeling their energies towards certain themes in life like power, creativity, sexuality, or love. The duads are layers of natal planets or the points that modify their energies. The interpretations of the twelfth harmonic readings significantly influence human behavior in many ways.

Apart from the Lots, six Hellenistic astrology techniques are also used for predictive purposes. They help people gain insight into aspects of their lives that are not readily apparent. While some of these techniques are ancient, they are used in other cultures and influence people's lives differently. It is essential to understand each technique before applying it to your life if you want to get meaningful results.

Chapter 11: Make Your Own Astrolabe

In the previous chapters, we discussed different Hellenistic techniques that astrologers used to perform different tasks, including the predictive functions based on celestial features. In this chapter, we will focus on astrolabes which are also fundamental tools for astrologers. We explain how Hellenistic astrologers used them and how the readers can apply the knowledge in their lives. Finally, you will find step-by-step instructions on how to create an astrolabe.

What Is an Astrolabe?

An astrolabe is a scientific tool used for observational purposes, calculating time, or generating the desired results using the universe. It enables astronomers to use the position of the Sun or prominent stars to calculate results that can be used for different purposes like navigation. Astrologers used astrolabes to gain insight into the image of the celestial sphere to help them learn various things about a person's life.

Astrolabes can be traced back to the 6th century and have been widely used since the early Middle Ages in different parts of the world. Around the 15th century, they were adopted by explorers, astrologers, mariners, and others to study celestial spheres. Astrolabes were viewed as the most commonly used astrological tool until the 1650s when more advanced devices were invented.

The astrolabe started as an engraved metal disc, but new features were added over time. Since its invention, there have been different types of astrolabes with smaller and bigger variants. They were used for various purposes, including navigation, calculating time, exploration, calculating horoscopes, astrology, prayer, astronomy, timekeeping, and creating birth charts.

How Hellenistic Astrologers Used Astrolabes

Hellenistic astrologers mainly used this instrument to study different aspects of birth charts. An astrolabe is a disc (Mater) that holds plates (Tympan) and can measure the specific location of the heavenly bodies. Above the tympan and mater is a rete (a "spider's web" in Latin, thus a sort of network) that can freely rotate, consisting of several pointers. These pointers were used to indicate the positions of the brightest stars in the sky.

There are many different shapes of pointers—balls, hands, leaves, stars, and many more. Using stars, you can rotate the pointer until the stars move over the projections. Each rotation denotes a day in the passage of time.

The astronomers assumed that the stars in the sky were positioned at an equal distance from the Earth when they mapped the heavens. Using this model, they created a two-dimensional representation of the celestial sphere – visible on astrolabes and star charts. The result produced a starry representation of a map on Earth. The front part of the astrolabe was used to show the map of the night sky that appeared in the form of a rotating net-like rete. Medieval writers described the rete as the spider.

The most crucial component of the traditional astrolabe is a circular metal plate with a diameter of about 6 inches. It can hang in a vertical position when suspended by a ring. The other side of the disc is black, consisting of several circle measurements like 360 degrees, 12 for months, 365 ¼ for days in a year, and others. The engravings were used for trigonometric calculations, and the outer circle on the astrolabe had 24 divisions representing the hours. Zodiacal constellations were used to create a calendar. The equator and tropics were carved in the center of the disc consisting of a celestial pole.

Another disc could be affixed to the front of the instrument and rotated. Several holes were made into the disc to allow the user to see through the body of the astrolabe. The cuts were explicitly meant for creating a map of the sky. They also included a broad annulus, flames, and tongues pointing to major stars in the sky. Thin engraved papers or discs were also used between the outer circle and the sky disc.

The astrolabe and its components were mainly used to measure distance and time by using the shadow cast by the alidade, also known as a gnomon. The gnomon produces a shadow from a conical-shaped feature on the circular disk's edge. This led to the formation of an angle equal to the difference between the altitude and time for that specific time of the day. The angle could be used to tell the difference in times of the day, so it helps the astrologers create a birth chart and mark dates. If one wanted to use the astrolabe to measure altitude, one had to determine the latitude first.

There were spikes on the rete that corresponded with the star positions. We can look to the dog's head as the position of the Dog Star (Sirius). It could also show the elliptical path of the sun concerning a star and how it moved through the zodiac signs.

Another critical aspect of the rete is that it consisted of a plate written with the projection of the sky above the observer at a specific latitude. This plate could be removed, and calibrated pieces are placed to measure different latitudes. The rotating rule fixed on the center of the astrolabe was mainly used for readings.

The astrolabe has a rotating bar at its back called the label or alidade, and it is used to measure the altitude of different elements above the horizon of various celestial bodies. The back part of the instrument consists of degrees that were used for taking measurements of the altitude. It is also engraved with zodiac signs and a calendar. The astrologers used these features to measure the positions of different objects in the sky.

Users can use data from the astrolabe to determine their position in time and space. This information played a critical role in astrology since it was used to determine answers to several questions about celestial issues. The data was also used as an inference to solve different problems encountered by people in their lives.

Astronomy has greatly influenced astrology as the measurements of the planets and stars has become more exact. The movement of these heavenly bodies can also be tracked more accurately. Astrolabes have been invaluable and have become more accurate across the ages.

Astrolabes were later adopted in different parts of the world, and they shaped the subject of astrology as we know it today. Although astrolabes are rarely used today, they are still quite accurate. You can make your instrument if you want to have a feel of how ancient astrologers conducted their work.

Conclusion

Since the beginning of time, we've been observing the sky, planets, and stars. Every civilization, along with its culture and traditions, was essentially brought to life when a group of people tried to make sense of the world in their own way. There is no better way to learn about the world than by seeking answers from the world itself, hence, the development of the study of astrology. Records of astrological practices date back to 30,000 to 10,000 B.C.E, meaning that our modern-day understanding of the field was shaped over eons.

At first, people used to view astrology in a deterministic light; they believed that natural laws encompass astrology influenced personal will, fate, living environment, etc. And these beliefs made sense because it was easier for them to align their lives to the Earth's natural cycles, considering their hunting-gathering, agricultural, and nomadic lifestyles.

The distinct studies of astronomy and astrology were regarded as the same field for several centuries. Besides the lack of modern-day technology and limited resources of the time, people believed that both areas of practice went hand-in-hand because of their superstitious beliefs. Eras ago, people's ability to survive depended on the general condition of nature. Many cultures thought that if the Gods were angry, they'd hold out on the rainfall to cause drought or instigate a flood to wipe out the crops. To prepare for the unknown, humans tried to deduce patterns by keeping track of the stars.

Humanity and technology evolved, and so did astrology. We've expanded our knowledge and elevated our consciousness throughout the centuries. The advancements we've made in fields like astronomy, science, mathematics, and technology have made it possible for us to have more control over our lives. Instead of needing astrology to survive and resorting to it from a place of fear, we now view it as a tool. Modern-day astrology is not only thought of as a way to enhance one's life (by learning how to use it to increase self-awareness, plan, improve relationships, etc.) but also as a means of entertainment by many.

Now that you've read this book, you know how astrology has evolved over the centuries to take the form we know today and have a great starting point if you wish to learn the ins and outs of astrology. It is also an ideal source of extensive knowledge for more experienced readers who wish to learn more. Either way, reading this book has given you a lot of insight into where many modern-day astrological practices and doctrines originate.

Bonus: Glossary of Astrological Terms

1. **Ascendant** - also referred to as the rising sign - is present on the cusp of the 1st house on a natal chart. It rises on the eastern horizon at the time of a person's birth.
2. **Astrological Compendium** - an astrological instrument used to tell the time and to perform various calculations. This contraption consists of a number of devices, including a sundial, a compass, lunar and solar volvelles, and a perpetual calendar.
3. **Benefic** - planets on your birth chart that have a positive or good influence on your life, and are said to bring fortune.
4. **Besiegement** - the placement of a planet between two malefic planets or their aspect points. Contrastingly, it can also be the placement of a planet between two benefic planets.
5. **Celestial bodies** - used to define objects in space, mainly planets (Mars, Jupiter, Saturn, Neptune, etc.), the Moon, or stars like the Sun.
6. **Constellations** - a group of stars forming recognizable patterns named after mythological figures.

7. **Culmination** - the transit of a celestial object across the meridian. Also known as meridian transits, these paths are circular in nature, and appear to be occurring because of the Earth's rotation.
8. **Cusp** - the natal chart consists of a total of 12 houses and 12 signs. The line that divides these signs or houses is referred to as the cusp. For instance, if your birth placement is on the cusp of Scorpio and Sagittarius, that means that the Sun was placed over this dividing line when you were born.
9. **Decan** - subdivisions of every zodiac sign to further narrow down personality traits and astrological information. Each zodiac sign is divided into three decans, each one being 10 degrees. Each of these decans also have planetary rulers, which makes them sub-rulers that give information about a specific persona.
10. **Descendant** - the opposite point of the ascendant, and also the point where the ecliptic sets. Mostly marks the end of the seventh house, and is one of the four points marking the natal chart.
11. **Delineation** - the interpretation of an astrological natal or birth chart. An astrologer usually does these, but it can also be computer generated these days.
12. **Depressed** - a planet is said to be depressed or in fall when it's in the zodiac exactly opposite to the one it rules. This essentially means that the ruling planet's influences block the planet's expression and general characteristics. Matters associated with this planet will likely bring you distress, worry, and a lack of appreciation.
13. **Eclipse** - when the Moon's orbit aligns with the Sun to create a lunation effect, it is known as an eclipse. Different types of eclipses take place, primarily lunar and solar eclipses. These occurrences are said to activate the lunar nodes, which can have a dramatic effect on our zodiacs. Depending on when these eclipses take place, they can majorly affect the aspects associated with the specific zodiac signs and bring considerable changes in your life.

14. **Equinox** – an equinox takes place when the Earth aligns its orbit directly around the sun. The Sun is thus positioned directly above the equator, resulting in the night and day being equal in length, i.e., 12 hours. This occurrence only occurs twice a year, namely on the 20th of March, known as the spring equinox, and the 23rd of September, the autumnal equinox.
15. **Exalted** – a planet is said to be exalted (or in domicile) when it is in the zodiac sign that it rules. It feels at home in its territory, and is thus comfortable expressing traits, and characteristics specific to the planet. Matters associated with this planet will bring you recognition and appreciation.
16. **Heliacal rising is** said to occur when the Sun moves so ahead of the star that the star becomes visible before the Sun rises in the morning. So, a heliacal rising will result in the star rising way before the Sun does every morning, and is visible until its light overwhelms it.
17. **Heliacal setting** – It is the opposite of heliacal rising. It takes place when the star sets after the sunset. This is when the Sun is far below the western horizon that it becomes briefly visible in the evening.
18. **Hermeticism** – hermetic thought is associated with the deity Hermes. According to this school of thought in astrology, the planet's movements are considered to have meaning beyond their physical sense and actually have metaphorical value. In this sense, these movements directly affect our lives in the sense that it doesn't dictate our actions, but it does influence our decisions.
19. **Horoscope** – A horoscope is another name for a natal chart and is used to describe an astrological chart representing the various positions of the luminaries, i.e., the Sun and the Moon, as well as the twelve planets at the time of an event. These positions are said to greatly influence said event.
20. **Latitude** – latitudes are used to describe the specific location with reference to the equator. Specifically, terrestrial latitude is used to define the angular distance of a location from north or south of the terrestrial equator. Similarly, the celestial latitude is defined as the angular distance of a

certain location from the south or north of the ecliptic.

21. **Longitude** - longitude goes hand in hand with latitude numerics to describe specific locations with reference to the equator. Namely, terrestrial longitudes are used to define the angular distance of a location east or west of the meridian, whereas celestial longitude defines the angular distance from a point along the ecliptic.

22. **Luminary body** - luminaries are used to describe celestial bodies that produce illumination and are considered the most important astronomical bodies. Luminaries translate to light sources; two primary luminary bodies include the sun, and the Moon. Stars are also considered to be important luminary bodies.

23. **Lunar cycle** - the lunar cycle follows the Moon's transit around the Earth's orbit. This movement around the Earth and the Sun creates a shadow on the Moon's far side, limiting the light that is reflected back to Earth. This results in the formation of specific shapes of the Moon. These shapes result in the moon's eight phases, including new Moon, waxing crescent, 1st quarter, waxing gibbous, full Moon, waning gibbous, 3rd quarter, and waning crescent. Each of these phases has its own meaning and affects the zodiacs.

24. **Malefic** - according to astrology, a malefic planet is said to bring misfortune and back luck to people born under it. Usually, Mars and Saturn are considered malefic planets, with Mars being the lesser between the two, and Saturn being the greater harbinger of bad luck.

25. **Meridian** - is the circle passing through the north and south of the horizon from a place of observation.

26. **Meridian distance** - is the distance of a planet or a celestial body from the meridian, and is measured in degrees, starting from right ascension to the celestial equator.

27. **Midheaven** - one of the four points on a natal chart, the midheaven point intersects the meridian vertically and is located on the upper end of this intersecting line.

28. **Planets** – celestial objects or heavenly bodies moving along fixed orbits on the axis of fixed stars, mainly, the Sun and the Moon. These include Mars, Venus, Jupiter, Saturn, Neptune, and Pluto.
29. **Prenatal lunation** – prenatal lunation charts are used to gain insight about our interactions in this world. These are for both new and full moons, and highlight our specific capabilities and characteristics.
30. **Retrograde** – planets are said to be in retrograde when they look like they start moving backwards, or in the opposite direction of their primary movement. This takes place among the five non-luminary planets and significantly affects zodiacs.
31. **Rising time is** the time required by a zodiac sign to rise over the horizon from a specific place of observation.
32. **Ruling planet** – ruling planets oversee various zodiac signs, and thus influence how a certain sign will interact. The ruling planet of a zodiac sign gives insight into a person's primary traits and personalities.
33. **Solstice** – the opposite of an equinox, a solstice takes place when the Sun reaches its most southward or northward excursion. Every year, two solstices take place, around 21st June (Summer Solstice) and 21st December (Winter Solstice).
34. **Triplicity** – triplicities are sub classifications of zodiac groups into a group 3 forming an equilateral triangle. These triplicities are thus ruled by three planets, primary, secondary, and participating rulers.
35. **Wicca** – Wiccan religion is classified as a modern Pagan religion. Experts categorize this school of thought as both a newly developed religious movement and as part of the esoteric religions.
36. **Ziggurat** – a structure, usually found in ancient Mesopotamia. It has a terraced structure of receding steps. This was most commonly utilized for viewing stars and other celestial bodies.

37. **Zodiac** – a total of twelve zodiacs originate from various constellations visible in the sky.

Here's another book by Mari Silva that you might like

Your Free Gift
(Only available for a limited time)

Thanks for getting this book! If you want to learn more about various spirituality topics, then join Mari Silva's community and get a free guided meditation MP3 for awakening your third eye. This guided meditation mp3 is designed to open and strengthen ones third eye so you can experience a higher state of consciousness. Simply visit the link below the image to get started.

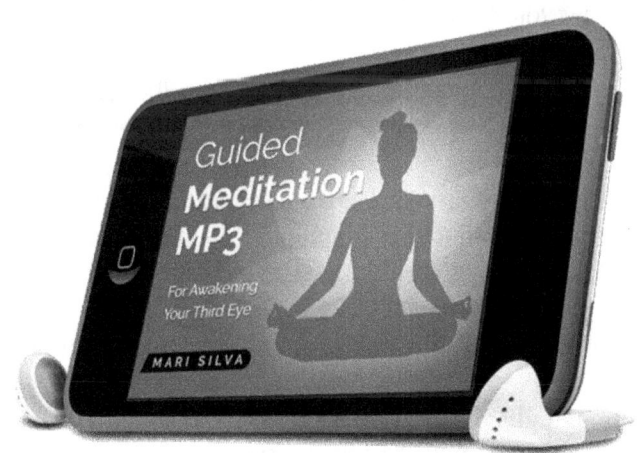

https://spiritualityspot.com/meditation

References

(N.d.). Mapsofindia.Com. https://www.mapsofindia.com/my-india/uncategorized/significance-of-astrology-in-our-lives#:~:text=It%20is%20an%20importance%20aspect,mishap%20related%20to%20planetary%20positions

Astrology: Ancient and modern. (n.d.). Classicsforall.Org.Uk. https://classicsforall.org.uk/reading-room/ad-familiares/astrology-ancient-and-modern

Cap, A. (2018, March 20). Why learn ancient astrology and its history? - Anthony cap. Medium. https://medium.com/@sevenstarsastrology/why-learn-ancient-astrology-and-its-history-b533c8d1c9e

Experience, N. S. L., & Marchesella, J. (2021, April 30). The benefits of astrology. Thriveglobal.Com. https://thriveglobal.com/stories/the-benefits-of-astrology/

Guest Column. (n.d.). 5 reasons to study astrology and how it can help your personal growth. Smudailycampus.Com. https://www.smudailycampus.com/sponsoredcontent/tactadv/5-reasons-to-study-astrology-and-how-it-can-help-your-personal-growth

Hammonds, O. (2014, August 5). 3 benefits of astrology. 3 Benefits Of. https://www.3benefitsof.com/3-benefits-of-astrology/

Macmillan, P. (2022, June 1). Why is astrology making a twenty-first-century comeback? Pan Macmillan. https://www.panmacmillan.com/blogs/lifestyle-wellbeing/the-popularity-of-astrology

Obert, C. (2011, October 12). Traditional and modern astrology. Student of Astrology. https://studentofastrology.com/2011/10/traditional-and-modern-astrology/

October. (2020, October 27). The three major forms of modern-day astrology. Brewminate: A Bold Blend of News and Ideas. https://brewminate.com/the-three-major-forms-of-modern-day-astrology/

Rubedo Press. (2019, January 5). The first five steps in learning traditional astrology. Rubedo Press. https://rubedo.press/propaganda/2018/12/21/first-five-steps

Schatsky, B. (2020, June 18). Astrology is a 21st-century trend. The Daily Northwestern. https://dailynorthwestern.com/2020/06/17/campus/astrology-an-unexpected-and-uniquely-modern-anchor-during-times-of-crisis/

Smallwood, C. (2019, October 17). Astrology in the age of uncertainty. New Yorker (New York, N.Y.: 1925). https://www.newyorker.com/magazine/2019/10/28/astrology-in-the-age-of-uncertainty

What are the differences between traditional and modern astrology? (n.d.). Quora. https://www.quora.com/What-are-the-differences-between-traditional-and-modern-astrology

About the name wandering stars — ☿ wandering stars. (n.d.). ☿ Wandering Stars. https://www.wandering-stars.net/about-the-name-wandering-stars

Adams, M. S. (2021, May 10). Mercury, the moon, and the great word. Interlochen Public Radio. https://www.interlochenpublicradio.org/2021-05-10/mercury-the-moon-and-the-great-word

All about mercury. (n.d.). Nasa.Gov. https://spaceplace.nasa.gov/all-about-mercury/en/

Amun. (n.d.). Egyptianmuseum.Org. https://egyptianmuseum.org/deities-amun

Ask-Aladdin. (n.d.). Isis Egyptian god – Isis the goddess of fertility – AskAladdin. Egypt Travel Experts. https://ask-aladdin.com/egypt-gods/isis/

AstroTwins. (2020, March 2). What are Benefic and Malefic Planets in Astrology? Astrostyle: Astrology and Daily, Weekly, Monthly Horoscopes by The AstroTwins. https://astrostyle.com/benefic-and-malefic-planets/

Beringer, B. (2021, August 26). Your Jupiter sign can tell you A lot about your personal growth. Bustle. https://www.bustle.com/life/jupiter-sign-meaning-astrology

Beringer-Tobing, B. (2022, March 24). What your Saturn sign means in astrology. POPSUGAR. https://www.popsugar.com/smart-living/saturn-sign-meaning-48757756

Bisht, N. (2022, March 31). Venus & Astrology: How the planet of love affects your love life. The Hindustan Times. https://www.hindustantimes.com/astrology/horoscope/venus-astrology-how-the-planet-of-love-affects-your-love-life-101648629708393.html

Brown, M. (2021, October 28). What your Mars sign means about your energy, anger, and sex life. Shape. https://www.shape.com/lifestyle/mind-and-body/astrology/mars-sign-meaning

Bunch, E. (2020, April 16). This is what it means when you have an exalted planet in your astrology chart. Well+Good. https://www.wellandgood.com/exalted-planet-astrology/

Cain, F. (2008, May 15). How Did Venus Get its Name? Universe Today. https://www.universetoday.com/14281/how-did-venus-get-its-name/

Cessna, A. (2009, July 8). Names of the planets. Universe Today. https://www.universetoday.com/34362/names-of-the-planets/

Coffey, J. (2008, June 4). Mars is Named After. Universe Today. https://www.universetoday.com/14825/mars-is-named-after/

Cradle of civilization. (2016, December 24). Cradle of Civilization. https://aratta.wordpress.com/2016/12/24/the-mythological-origin-of-mercury/

Crane, L. (2016, April 4). Wandering stars: A brief history of defining 'planet' –. Lateral Magazine. http://www.lateralmag.com/articles/issue-9/wandering-stars-a-brief-history-of-defining-planet

Davies, W. (Originally published: March 22, 2018). Mercury is entering retrograde again. This is why so many people care. Time. https://time.com/5207161/mercury-retrograde-astrology-history/

Deimos, moon of Mars – the Solar System on sea and sky. (n.d.). Seasky.Org. http://www.seasky.org/solar-system/mars-deimos.html

Dhankher, N. (2021, September 12). Jupiter's Retrograde Transit In Capricorn 2021: How to tap into its abundance. The Hindustan Times. https://www.hindustantimes.com/astrology/your-fortune-today/jupiters-retrograde-transit-in-capricorn-2021-how-to-tap-into-its-abundance-101631343877265.html

Early Times. (n.d.). Nasa.Gov. https://mars.nasa.gov/allaboutmars/mystique/history/early/

Editors, C. R. (2018). Thoth: The history and legacy of the ancient Egyptian god who maintains the universe. Createspace Independent Publishing Platform.

ESO. (n.d.). ESO https://www.eso.org/public/outreach/eduoff/vt-2004/Background/Infol2/EIS-D9.html

Exalted and debilitated planets. (2016, February 20). AstrologerPanditJi.Com. https://www.astrologerpanditji.com/page25.htm

Francos, E. (2022, January 19). What does your Saturn sign mean in astrology? YourTango. https://www.yourtango.com/2019328839/astrology-saturn-natal-chart-meaning-each-zodiac-sign-house

Grossman, L. (2016). What if... we put a colony on Mars? New Scientist (1971), 232(3100), 38. https://doi.org/10.1016/s0262-4079(16)32131-5

Hall, M. (2007, April 8). Mercury in Astrology. LiveAbout. https://www.liveabout.com/mercury-in-astrology-206363

How did Mars and its moons get their names? (n.d.). Cool Cosmos. https://coolcosmos.ipac.caltech.edu/ask/86-How-did-Mars-and-its-moons-get-their-names-

How did Mercury get its name? (n.d.). Cool Cosmos. https://coolcosmos.ipac.caltech.edu/ask/33-How-did-Mercury-get-its-name-

How did Saturn get its name? (n.d.). Cool Cosmos. https://coolcosmos.ipac.caltech.edu/ask/115-How-did-Saturn-get-its-name-

How did the planets get their names? (n.d.). Cool Cosmos. https://coolcosmos.ipac.caltech.edu/ask/196-How-did-the-planets-get-their-names-

How did Venus get its name? (n.d.). Cool Cosmos. https://coolcosmos.ipac.caltech.edu/ask/41-How-did-Venus-get-its-name-

What is Jupiter? https://www.nasa.gov/audience/forstudents/5-8/features/nasa-knows/what-is-jupiter-58.html

In Depth. (n.d.-a). NASA Solar System Exploration. https://solarsystem.nasa.gov/planets/venus/in-depth/

In Depth. (n.d.-b). NASA Solar System Exploration. https://solarsystem.nasa.gov/planets/saturn/in-depth/

Interesting facts about Venus. (n.d.). Rmg.Co.Uk https://www.rmg.co.uk/stories/topics/interesting-facts-about-venus

Jawer, J. (2018, January 6). Exalted planets in astrology. Tarot.Com. https://www.tarot.com/astrology/exalted-planets

Jupiter – the generous planet of wealth and wisdom. (2021, October 6). GaneshaSpeaks. https://www.ganeshaspeaks.com/astrology/planets/jupiter/

Jupiter, king of the gods, in Astrology/zodiac. (2015, April 13). Cafeastrology.Com; Cafe Astrology .com. https://cafeastrology.com/jupiter.html

Kedziora-Chudczer, L. (2019, September 9). Curious Kids: why does Saturn have rings? The Conversation. http://theconversation.com/curious-kids-why-does-saturn-have-rings-121433

Kelly, A. (2018, July 31). What the position of Venus in your birth chart means for you. Allure. https://www.allure.com/story/venus-birth-chart-planet-of-love

Machholz, D., Whitt, K. K., & Byrd, D. (2021, November 28). Why is Venus so bright? EarthSky | Updates on Your Cosmos and World; EarthSky. https://earthsky.org/astronomy-essentials/why-is-venus-so-bright/

Mark, J. J. (2017). Nergal. World History Encyclopedia. https://www.worldhistory.org/Nergal/

Mars, god of war, in Astrology/zodiac. (2015a, April 13). Cafeastrology.Com; Cafe Astrology .com. https://cafeastrology.com/mars.html

Mars, god of war, in Astrology/zodiac. (2015b, April 13). Cafeastrology.Com; Cafe Astrology .com. https://cafeastrology.com/mars.html

Mercury, messenger of the gods, in Astrology/zodiac. (2015a, April 19). Cafeastrology.Com; Cafe Astrology .com. https://cafeastrology.com/mercury.html

Mercury, messenger of the gods, in Astrology/zodiac. (2015b, April 19). Cafeastrology.Com; Cafe Astrology .com. https://cafeastrology.com/mercury.html

Oomen, M. (2022, March 15). Find the Benefic and Malefic Planets in Birth chart. Astrology Articles | Clickastro Blog. https://www.clickastro.com/blog/planets-in-birth-chart/

Pappas, S. (2012, June 5). Five odd facts you might not know about Venus. NBC News. https://www.nbcnews.com/id/wbna47694036

Phobos, moon of Mars – the solar system on sea and sky. (n.d.). Seasky.Org. http://www.seasky.org/solar-system/mars-phobos.html

Planet Mercury. (n.d.). Urban Astrologer https://www.urban-astrologer.com/planet-mercury.html

Planet Mercury In Astrology. (n.d.). Astrosage.Com. https://www.astrosage.com/planet/mercury/

Planets & astrology: Saturn. (2016, November 8). Astrostyle: Astrology and Daily, Weekly, Monthly Horoscopes by The AstroTwins; The AstroTwins. https://astrostyle.com/astrology-planets-saturn/

Retrogrades: When planets go "backward" in astrology. (2013, October 19). Astrostyle: Astrology and Daily, Weekly, Monthly Horoscopes by The AstroTwins; The AstroTwins. https://astrostyle.com/learn-astrology/retrogrades/

Saturn. (n.d.). NASA Solar System Exploration. https://solarsystem.nasa.gov/planets/saturn/overview/

Saturn. (2017, February 23). Greek Gods & Goddesses. https://greekgodsandgoddesses.net/gods/saturn/

Saturn in Astrology, zodiac. (2015, April 19). Cafeastrology.Com; Cafe Astrology .com. https://cafeastrology.com/saturn.html

Saturn: Jewel of the solar system. (n.d.). Exploratorium.Edu. https://www.exploratorium.edu/saturn/saturn.html

Sesay, A. (2020, October 20). Your Saturn sign is your cosmic teacher—here's how to find yours. Cosmopolitan. https://www.cosmopolitan.com/lifestyle/a34426595/saturn-sign-meaning/

Stardust, L. (2021, June 11). The best way to get through Mercury retrograde is to do nothing at all. Oprah Daily. https://www.oprahdaily.com/entertainment/a36593904/what-is-mercury-retrograde-meaning-astrology/

Student video: Mars in a minute: Is mars really red? (2020, December 24). Nasa.Gov. https://www.jpl.nasa.gov/edu/learn/video/mars-in-a-minute-is-mars-really-red/

Thomas, K. (2021a, October 22). Here's what a retrograde in astrology means and how it affects you. New York Post. https://nypost.com/article/retrograde-meaning-explained/

Thomas, K. (2021b, December 24). What your Jupiter sign means in astrology and what it reveals about you. New York Post. https://nypost.com/article/jupiter-sign-meaning/

Venus. (n.d.). NASA Solar System Exploration. https://solarsystem.nasa.gov/planets/venus/overview/

Venus astrology symbol – characteristics, planet energy and more. (2018, January 22). Labyrinthos. https://labyrinthos.co/blogs/astrology-horoscope-zodiac-signs/venus-astrology-symbol-characteristics-planet-energy

Ward, K. (2020, April 7). How to find your Mercury sign, AKA the chatty part of your birth chart. Cosmopolitan. https://www.cosmopolitan.com/lifestyle/a32055636/what-is-mercury-sign/

www.ingramcontent.com/pod-product-compliance
Lightning Source LLC
Chambersburg PA
CBHW071901090426
42811CB00004B/694